Restoring Confidence In The Financial System

Hh | Harriman House

Harriman House is one of the UK's leading independent publishers of financial and business books. Our catalogue covers personal finance, stock marking investing and trading, current affairs, business and economics. For more details go to:

www.harriman-house.com

Restoring Confidence In The Financial System

See-through leverage: a powerful new tool for revealing and managing risk

by Sean Tully and Richard Bassett

HARRIMAN HOUSE LTD

3A Penns Road
Petersfield
Hampshire
GU32 2EW
GREAT BRITAIN

Tel: +44 (0)1730 233870
Fax: +44 (0)1730 233880
Email: enquiries@harriman-house.com
Website: www.harriman-house.com

First published by Harriman House Ltd in Great Britain

Copyright © Sean Tully and Richard Bassett 2010

Sean Tully and Richard Bassett assert the moral right to be identified as the authors of
this work under the Copyright, Design and Patents Act 1988.

978-1906659-66-0

British Library Cataloguing in Publication Data
A CIP catalogue record for this book can be obtained from the British Library.

Printed in the United States of America

To the scientists and clinicians of the Kidneeds sponsored Dense Deposit Disease Focus Group, who dedicate their time to search for a cure to this disease; to the hundreds of people who contribute to support their efforts, and to the patients with this condition, whose courage is inspirational. A portion of the proceeds of this book will be used to support this search for a cure.

Contents

Acknowledgements

The authors wish to thank a number of individuals for their valuable insights and criticisms, namely: Igor Yalovenko, Michael Regan, Darren Smith, David Aragon, David Pfeiffer, Thomas McCaffery, Stefan Dreesbach, Ali Bajwa, Hope Fider Tully, Michael Tully and Patrick Tully. Thanks are also due to Crispin Drummond, Mark Philpot, John Cook, John Stevens and Ned Falconer who all contributed in different ways to the authors' insights and the overall project. The book would never have been possible without the tireless efforts of our agent, Kate Hordern. Most importantly, the work of our editor Craig Pearce, and the staff at Harriman House, was an enormous help in turning our rough manuscript into a readable, easy-to-use text. Nonetheless, the authors of course take full responsibility for any errors.

The authors also wish to thank their families and friends for their strong support and encouragement, especially during the nights, weekends and holidays during which the text was written. Sean especially wishes to thank Hope, Kristina and Alessandra Tully.

The authors also wish to acknowledge the following:

Extract from *In an Uncertain World* by Robert E. Rubin and Jacob Weisberg, reproduced with the permission of Random House Trade, USA.

Extract from *The (Mis)behaviour of Markets* by Benoit Mandelbrot and Richard L. Hudson, reproduced with the permission of Basic Books, USA.

Extract from *The New Paradigm for Financial Markets* by George Soros, reproduced with the permission of Public Affairs, USA.

Extract from *The Age of Turbulence* by Alan Greenspan, reproduced with the permission of Penguin Press (London), Penguin Group Inc (USA), and Williams & Connolly (USA).

Extract from *Fool's Gold* by Gillian Tett, reproduced with the permission of Little, Brown (London), The Free Press, a Division of Simon & Schuster, Inc. (USA), and International Creative Management (USA). © 2009 by Gillian Tett. All rights reserved.

Extract from *Stabilizing an Unstable Economy* by Hyman P. Minsky reproduced with the permission of The McGraw Hill Companies, Inc. © Hyman P. Minsky 2008.

Preface

What this book covers

This book advances a single, unifying approach to understanding all major aspects of the 2007-2009 financial crisis and offers clear practical tools for addressing it, in order to help ensure the same situation does not occur again.

It is our view that at the heart of the 2007-2009 crisis was a conceptual error in the way risk was viewed and measured since the advent of Basel I more than 20 years ago. We also make the case that this crisis was driven by the same risk management errors as were evident in previous crises.

The new conceptual approach advanced here resolves the paradoxes and explains the themes of this crisis with a single unifying concept – see-through leverage (STL) – the implementation of which will prevent similar crises from ever occurring again.

With STL, the insightful concepts of such thought-leaders as Nassim Taleb, Benoit Mandelbrot and Hyman Minsky are translated into an instrument that can be applied to decision-making on a daily basis. For the first time, a new generalised definition of leverage that ties all of these strands together is introduced.

We examine the following points:

- How the events of the recent crisis can be explained.

- How the recent crisis has many similarities with previous crises such as the 1929 Wall Street crash, the Japanese financial crisis and the LTCM crisis.

- How so many AAA-rated securities could suddenly become worthless.

- Why certain highly rated, well-capitalised banks and insurance companies came to the brink of collapse and suddenly required government assistance.

- How funds that had strong consistent returns suddenly became valueless.

- How AAA-rated monoline insurers and highly rated credit derivative product companies were suddenly on the brink of default.

- How so many regulators, bankers and politicians who were sensitive to risk missed the iceberg of systemic risk the global financial system was about to hit.

- How concepts introduced by Hyman Minsky, Benoit Mandelbrot, Nassim Taleb and George Soros relate to the crisis and how their insights can be incorporated into the new measurement tool introduced here, which can then be used to prevent another similar crisis from recurring.

- How misuse of the Nobel Prize-winning mathematics at the foundation of current regulations, much of modern finance and ratings, also lay at the foundation of previous crises.

A new approach

The new approach advanced here defines leverage for all new products, especially those of the shadow banking system, asset-backed securities and derivatives, in a way which is consistent with the traditional definition of leverage, but which is also independent of predictions of future market price changes and future loss distributions.

Once this new language of risk is created, explained and clarified, the conceptual error that was caused by over reliance on certain risk measures, which ignored this new paradigm, becomes clear.

After showing in detail how this conceptual error led to the financial crisis, the book aims to lead the way forward for all participants in global financial markets, informing them how to navigate uncertainty. To this end a new family of risk indices is introduced, which will allow investors, regulators and rating agencies the opportunity to have restored confidence in their daily activities.

The book introduces first the concept of *simple tranche leverage*, or STL(0), a new risk index for debt securities and, in particular, simple asset-backed securities (ABS). Next, this concept is extended to *see-through leverage*, or STL(X), a new risk index for securities and, in particular, re-securitised ABS.

Finally, we introduce *enhanced see-through leverage*, or ESTL(X), which also includes the leverage of the borrower into the final all-comprehensive risk index.

Each of these new risk indices (STL(0), STL(X) and ESTL(X)[1]) are referred to in general as the family of STL risk indices. In the case of a structure with just

---

[1] Patent application pending.

one layer, which is the typical example used in this book, STL = STL(0) = STL(X), so the terms are interchangeable.

Who this book is for

This book is intended for investors, risk managers, bankers, regulators and politicians. It is written so as to be easily accessible to readers who are informed on the crisis and relatively numerate – they will be able to follow the authors' arguments with regard to the new language of risk and the new family of risk indices called STL. A glossary appended at the end of the book is also a useful guide for those unfamiliar with the terms of structured finance. At their first mention in the text, relevant terms are **emboldened** to indicate their inclusion in the glossary.

How this book is structured

This book is organised as follows:

Chapter one outlines the general political and regulatory events which preceded the 2007-2009 crisis.

Chapter two delves into the detail of the salient points of Basel I and Basel II banking regulations. The reader will quickly realise how naïve the approach of these accords was to financial risk; risk that can now be exposed by the family of STL risk indices.

Chapter three shows how this regulatory environment, in conjunction with the mathematics used by the rating agencies, led to the birth and enormous growth of new products and the shadow banking system, and a massive increase in financial risk which went unmeasured or – as we argue – was incorrectly measured.

This account of the history leading up to the crisis and exploration of the failures of the existing regulatory framework provides a useful explanatory background, but some readers may wish to move straight to the following chapters, which are more analytical, and introduce the STL concept.

Chapter four introduces the new language of risk, and the new family of STL risk indices.

Chapter five then shows how to apply this new family of risk indices to the financial markets and banking system, with many examples.

Finally, chapter six describes how this family of risk indices might be used by regulators in order to ensure the global financial system never again falls into this same abyss.

At the beginning of each chapter there is a summary section, laying out the main points covered within that chapter.

The aims of this book

It is hoped that at the very least this book will inform a debate which shows no sign of diminishing in either intensity or importance. We strongly believe the family of STL risk indices should become a daily instrument of risk measurement for investors, regulators and rating agencies alike, distinguishing between strong triple-A assets and those which, though labelled AAA, fall far short of the general expectations associated with that term.

STL will help distinguish between truly well-capitalised banks and weak, cyclically risky ones. STL will reduce the opportunity for bubbles to occur, and will help prevent systemic crises.

Introduction

"Our world is broken – and I honestly do not know what is going to replace it."

Bernie Sucher, Merrill Lynch, *WSJ*, 14/12/2009

The morning of 16 October 1555 was bright. In front of Balliol College, Oxford, the fires were being prepared to receive two famous heretics who would be burnt at the stake. England in the 1550s was turbulent, bloody and violent. Under Queen Mary the old religion of England was being reintroduced, and prominent members of the clergy who supported the break with Rome initiated by Henry VIII were being arrested and executed. This morning it was the turn of Latimer and, most gifted of the pair, a young Cambridge graduate who had been King Henry's private chaplain; Nicholas Ridley. His death, if contemporary accounts are to be believed, would be especially dreadful. For the Northumbrian Ridley, the fires burnt extremely slowly.

Nearly 500 years later it was to be a descendant of Nicholas Ridley's, Matt Ridley, who would, as chairman of Northern Rock, take the heat in the first bailout of a British bank since 1866 (fortunately in Matt Ridley's case, the heat was only metaphorical). The British media took some pleasure in depicting the heir to a viscountcy and generous estate as some remote landed toff whose financial credentials were non-existent.

In fact Ridley, like so many of his family, combined substantial intellectual gifts with a progressive mindset far removed from most of his landowning contemporaries. His nemesis had been the quiet revolution which in less than ten years had transformed the sleepy, relatively straightforward craft of banking into a branch of applied mathematics in which credit risk depended no longer on a bank manager's familiarity with a customer but on complex, computer-driven systems. If the central bankers gathered in Basel found it difficult to keep up, then the old British tradition of the gifted amateur suddenly looked highly exposed.

Needless to say the developments were not recognised for the risks they entailed but rather the evidence of progress they appeared to offer. Regulators appreciated the shedding of credit exposures by banks, since the US savings and loan crises of the 1980s had demonstrated the dangers of loan sector concentrations and encouraged banks to diversify their exposures. In the spring of 2006 no less a body than the International Monetary Fund noted that the dispersion of credit risk could be greeted as positive news for "it had helped to make the banking and overall financial system more resilient." The bankers, for their part, received fees at every step of the slicing and dicing chain. As the banks shed credit risk, more and more credit could in turn be pumped into the economy, creating even more banking fees. At Northern Rock in 2007, someone pointed out to the bank's board that they could extend three times more loans per unit of capital than five years earlier, as mortgages were securitised and ever more complex products were created in a mad scramble for financial innovation.[2]

> **❝ Developments in the craft of banking were not recognised for the risks they entailed but rather the evidence of progress they appeared to offer. ❞**

One popular method used to achieve this was the **collateralised debt obligation (CDO)**, which arose as bundles of mortgage-linked bonds were packaged into instruments that tended to be sold to off-balance-sheet entities known as **structured investment vehicles (SIVs)**. The value of these instruments, however, was derived from complex computer models which failed to take into account the amount of leverage that was often devised from modest capital. As Gillian Tett has written, "a set of innovations which was designed to create freer markets actually produced an opaque world in which risk was being concentrated – and in ways almost nobody understood."[3] We will show that the risks of CDOs and SIVs are remarkably similar to the risks incurred by some of the investment trusts involved in the stock market crash of 1929, and the collapse of Long-Term Capital Management (LTCM).

Rating agencies facilitated this distribution of risk and admitted that it would take their most sophisticated computers more than a week to assess the risks of some CDOs.[4] As we show in the later part of the book, they missed the fact

---

[2] *Financial Times*, 09/11/2008.

[3] Gillian Tett, *Fool's Gold* (Little, Brown, 2009).

[4] *Financial Times*, 04/04/2009.

that these instruments can promote a dramatic increase in leverage; but that did not deter investors from buying these complex products, because they trusted the risk assessment of the credit ratings.

In spring 2007 the faith in these assumptions and calculations began to come under heightened scrutiny. This began in the US as delinquencies began to rise sharply on US subprime mortgages. Some banks, such as HSBC, announced dramatic increases in mortgage loss provisions. Agencies including Standard & Poor's cut ratings for mortgage-linked products and faith in their modelling began to be questioned. In the early part of 2007, BBB-rated subprime mortgage price indices had begun to falter and by August AAA-rated indices faltered as well.

Almost immediately **money market** investors took fright and the practice of buying **commercial paper** (CP) issued by SIVs began to come dramatically to a halt. As the SIVs came under scrutiny so did the entire world of shadow banking and off-balance-sheet vehicles. This, however, had an impact on the real banking world as there was a growing realisation that many banks were exposed to SIVs. Fund managers, who should have perhaps known better, expressed dismay at the scope at which the SIV model had been developed by banks. As so many of the instruments had been highly rated, the element of risk came as a shock.

The attitude towards some of the most highly rated structured products was best summed up by the UBS chairman Peter Kurer, who stated at the height of the crisis: "We never paid much attention to these because our risk managers said they were all rated triple A." As 2007 ended and 2008 began, billions of dollars of structured credit

> **What brought the best brains and the old guard down was the deadly combination of low probability and high impact.**

assets started to be written down. The term 'bad bank' had yet to be coined but 'risk shield' and other phrases began to gain currency as banks scrambled to isolate the risk from their balance sheets.

Several countries moved to increase, or in some cases fully guarantee, retail bank deposits in order to prevent runs. The models which had so plausibly labelled two-thirds of these structured assets AAA were perceived to have failed. As Joshua Rosner, the US economist, stated: "This was the era when models failed." Faith in the banks failed; trust in the rating agencies evaporated and confidence, perhaps the most crucial component of market sentiment, was eroded. All that was missing was a large bank failure and the US proceeded to provide this in the form of the collapse of Lehman Brothers. Most funding markets seized up and a few weeks later no less a person than the Governor of the Bank of England, Mervyn King, said that the system was "on the precipice".

In order to restore the money market's functionality, the governments of the US and other major states had to step in. In the US stress testing by the Treasury began, while in the UK the state insured the banks against losses on toxic assets.

As Paul Volcker, the former head of the Federal Reserve, noted: "Simply stated; the bright new financial system – for all its talented participants, for all its rich rewards – has failed the test of the marketplace."[5]

A Bank of England financial stability paper of February 2009 made the more telling point that the failure was partly attributable to "disaster myopia", a tendency to underestimate risks.[6] And, in another implied reference to Nassim Taleb's black swan thesis, a lack of awareness of network externalities was also blamed.

Taleb describes a black swan thus:

> First, it is an outlier, as it lies outside the realm of regular expectations, because nothing in the past can convincingly point to its possibility. Second, it carries an extreme impact. Third, in spite of its outlier status, human nature makes us concoct explanations for its occurrence after the fact, making it explainable and predictable.[7]

In the end what brought the best brains and the old guard down was the deadly combination of low probability and high impact, both of which are the hallmarks of the black swan. As Taleb notes:

> The application of the science of uncertainty to real world problems has had ridiculous effects. I have been privileged to see it in finance and economics. Go ask your portfolio manager for his definition of 'risk' and odds are that he will supply one with a measure that

---

[5] John Brinsley and Anthony Massucci, 'Volcker Says Fed's Bear Loan Stretches Legal Power', Bloomberg, 08/04/2009.

[6] Andrew Haldane, 'Why Banks Failed the Stress Test',
www.bankofengland.co.uk/publications/speeches/2009/speech374.pdf

[7] Nassim Taleb, *The Black Swan* (Penguin Books, 2007), p. xvii.

excludes the possibility of the black swan – hence one that has no better predictive value for assessing the total risks than astrology.[8]

Although there are many different risk measures applied in financial risk management, many widely used measures (such as probability of default, expected loss and VaR) are based on predictions of future probability distributions. As we will see throughout this book, future probability distributions of social phenomena such as markets are in general unknown and are impossible to estimate accurately.

The concept of the family of STL risk indices is introduced here as a suggested method for addressing this inconsistency between the true nature of the financial markets on the one side and established risk measurement practices on the other.

---

[8] Ibid.

1

Brave New World

"It is important for capital to be productively deployed. It cannot just be stashed under the mattress."

Alan Greenspan

"Personally I think Margaret Thatcher did wonders for the City of London. Big Bang broke up the old network of lazy individuals who had all been to school together."

Ken Livingstone

Chapter summary

- Margaret Thatcher and Ronald Reagan unleashed huge amounts of human potential by reducing regulations and allowing market-based competition to regulate how business was done.

- Mathematicians and financial engineers entered the congenial world of banking and changed it dramatically. Powerful models based on simplifying assumptions became the tools of finance.

- Regulators and political leaders were outwardly very risk-sensitive, but via the *great moderation* they potentially increased capitalism's susceptibility to risk. Even more so, they missed the systemic risk that was progressively building up.

- Several historical systemic risk events were driven by increases in leverage, namely the 1929 Wall Street crash, the worldwide crash of 1987, the Japanese financial crisis of the 1990s, the 1994 derivatives 'blow-up' and the LTCM crisis of the late 1990s.

- Increasing leverage based upon predicted loss distributions increases return on capital and increases systemic risk. The short-term interests of bank equity holders and the long-term interests of bank regulators became diametrically opposed.

- A conceptual gap in the measurement of risk went on for many years, and caused the credit crisis of 2007-2009. That gap is the failure to acknowledge leverage as a primary source of systemic risk.

Big Bang: the City reborn

The early 1970s was a time of seismic events for the City of London. A sea of bowler hats might still be visible most mornings flowing across London Bridge. Detachable collars and umbrellas might still have pointed to a hierarchy as rigid as the narrow group of educational establishments whose alumni comprised most of the City's senior management. But underneath this veneer near-revolutionary changes were being contemplated.

When the Bretton Woods system of fixed exchange rates collapsed in the early 1970s, a new orthodoxy rose from the ruins: namely, that monetary flexibility was the primary mechanism for achieving sustainable growth. This economic doctrine was epitomised by former Federal Reserve boss Alan Greenspan's now infamous 'put': no matter what goes wrong, the Fed will rescue the economy by creating enough cheap money. Greenspan was aware of the limits to his knowledge and that the known unknowns and the unknown unknowns had a very good chance of coming back to haunt him, but no one, least of all those who worked on the new instruments which made up the **shadow banking system**, would have thought that the problems that were to occur could ever take place.

Greenspan nurtured the idea of unfettered capitalism, and this doctrine allowed great strides in finance and technology. However, a combination of events allowed this economic doctrine – when allied with the inbuilt propensity to seek ever more inventive ways of providing financial services – to go too far. To find out how this happened we need to return to those days when, under the surface of on the whole controlled post-imperial decline, the entire way in which money and finance were transacted in the City was overhauled by a radical injection of new blood. The City, more than Wall Street, was going to undergo a fundamental transformation with this process.

Political background to the changes

Today it is convenient to turn a blind eye to the weaknesses and chaos which were the hallmarks of the Western economies in the 1970s. In the US, the Carter administration brought American pride and prestige to an all-time low. America's foreign policy was a mess, and America's economy was in decline. Inflation hit 13.5% and US output, like the dollar, began to spiral downwards.

In the UK, the humiliation of the three-day week, daily power cuts and photographs of the vans parked in Threadneedle Street ready to transfer the

Bank of England's gold supplies to Switzerland fuelled rumours of a coup d'etat. Not only did retired colonels talk privately of seizing the BBC, Whitehall and the Bank of England, Colonel David Stirling, founder of the SAS, formed a secret group to infiltrate trade union picket lines in the event of industrial unrest. The FT30 crashed though a thousand, breaching the low point of the previous bear market of 1968-71 for the first time since the index was introduced in 1935. Jim Slater told Slater Walker's annual meeting that "cash is the best investment now". Meanwhile Russia, sensing the weakness of the West, prepared to invade Afghanistan.

All these events proved to be the nails in the coffin of Keynesian liberalism. If some historians saw the era until 1979 as a golden age, others recall a country whose once proud traditions of independence and leadership had been fatally compromised. If Britain was not to be destined for inexorable decline, drastic measures would have to be taken.

The liberal experiment had failed and an alternative paradigm was eagerly sought. This paradigm would roll back the activities and regulations of the state, free the market and reclaim the liberties of the individual allegedly trammelled by a bloated state bureaucracy. The key to this was monetary flexibility. But it would be accompanied by the fiscal outriders of lower direct taxation; the scaling back of capital gains taxes and a massive boost to the financial services industry and the City of London.

Friedrich von Hayek

The election of Margaret Thatcher in the UK, and later Ronald Reagan in the US, provided a political framework to achieve these changes. As ideological ammunition, both turned to the hitherto almost forgotten Austrian school of economics and in particular the writings of Friedrich von Hayek. In 1974, Hayek jointly won the Nobel Prize for economics, stimulating a revival of interest in the Austrian school. Read in the context of the faltering of Western economies in the 1970s, Hayek's 1944 book *The Road To Serfdom* shone a stark light on these economic problems, criticising as it did centrally planned economies and drawing chilling conclusions from its contemporary context of totalitarianism in Germany and the Soviet Union.

Today, it is argued that Hayek was not the undiluted advocate of laissez-faire capitalism which so many interpreted him to be. He wrote that, "Governments have a role to play in the economy through the monetary system, work-hours regulation and social welfare." However, both in the US and the UK, his writings became part of the ideological foundation of the conservative governments. Margaret Thatcher famously banged a copy of his writings on her desk after she was elected Conservative leader, saying "This is what we believe in."[9]

At a stroke, Mrs Thatcher had the intellectual firepower she needed to accomplish far-reaching reforms with regard to the City of London and the way finance had been conducted there since the second world war. At the same time, she waged a bitter war of attrition against the miners and the trade unions, causing dramatic change in the working practices of the country. Ironically in Austria, where socialist governments held sway, her policies were seen in a more critical light. Austrian Chancellor Bruno Kreisky noted: "I am a great admirer of Mrs Thatcher but her policies would not work here. They were tried out before" – an oblique reference to the troubles Austria experienced in the thirties.

Reagan and the United States

In the US, David Stockman, President Reagan's advisor, was no less a devotee of Hayek.[10] Ronald Reagan took over the White House in 1981 and for the next eight years he led America, and to some extent the world, with his own brand of American conservatism. Reagan fuelled growth with the largest tax cuts in American history and supported unfettered entrepreneurship in every way. During this time, Paul Volcker, the former Chase Manhattan banker, was Chairman of the Federal Reserve.

Having been appointed by President Jimmy Carter, Paul Volcker inherited a US economy with a high and rising inflation rate. He took the reins of monetary policy and broke the back of insidious inflation – which reached over 13% in 1981 – by raising rates to over 20%, causing the highest unemployment levels since the Great Depression. Volcker performed well the single hardest task faced by any Fed Chairman; that of taking the punch bowl away.

According to Economics Nobel Laureate Joseph Stiglitz:

> Volcker had done what central bankers are supposed to do. On his watch, inflation had been brought down from more than 11% to

---

[9] John Ranelagh, *Thatcher's People: An Insider's Account of the Politics, the Power, and the Personalities* (HarperCollins, 1991).

[10] Alan Ebenstein, *Friedrich Hayek: A Biography* (University of Chicago Press, 2001), p. 208.

under 4%. In the world of central banking, that should have earned him a grade of A+++ and assured his re-appointment. But Volcker also understood that financial markets need to be regulated. Reagan wanted someone who did not believe any such thing, and he found him in a devotee of the objectivist philosopher and free-market zealot Ayn Rand.[11]

Reagan was surely relieved with Volcker's success in reducing inflation, but he was apparently even more interested in doing everything possible to foster entrepreneurial spirit. Reagan wanted more freedom and less regulation.

On 12 June 1987, towards the end of his administration, Reagan summed up the new world he had been working to create in a famous speech at the Brandenburg Gate:

> We welcome change and openness; for we believe that freedom and security go together, that the advance of human liberty can only strengthen the cause of world peace. There is one sign the Soviets can make that would be unmistakeable, that would advance dramatically the cause of freedom and peace. General Secretary Gorbachev, if you seek peace, if you seek prosperity for the Soviet Union and Eastern Europe, if you seek liberalization: come here to this gate! Mr Gorbachev, open this gate! Mr Gorbachev, tear down this wall![12]

Reagan was alluding to the tearing down of the walls of oppressive totalitarianism in order to unleash the human spirit and allow freedom and individual initiative to reign. This was exactly the environment needed for fostering the new technologies which would be created over the next 20 years – in the West as well as the East – and which would change the way of life for the better for much of the world's population.

Two months after this speech, in one of his most significant decisions, Reagan appointed Alan Greenspan successor to Volcker as Chairman of the Federal Reserve.

Greenspan had worked in the Ford White House and was a known libertarian, and supporter and friend of author Ayn Rand. In his memoirs, Greenspan recalled his relationship with Rand and her objectivist philosophy with the

---

[11] Joseph Stiglitz, 'Capitalist Fools', *Vanity Fair*, January 2009.

[12] Ronald Reagan speech, Remarks on East-West Relations at the Brandenburg Gate in West Berlin, 12 June 1987, www.reagan.utexas.edu/archives/speeches/1987/061287d.htm

words: "I still found the broader philosophy of unfettered market competition compelling as I do to this day."[13]

For Greenspan, like Reagan, it was important to allow entrepreneurs free reign. This free will and free choice supported risk taking in order to maximise innovation and growth, and in this environment restraint and regulation needed to be scattered to the four winds. The subsequent unleashing of human talent and innovation became the hallmark of the 1980s and 1990s.

Change gathers pace in the City

Two years after Reagan's Berlin speech Gorbachev did indeed open the gate and the Berlin Wall was torn down; the population of Eastern Europe was now free to choose and innovate. This pioneering spirit was also evident in America where, during the late 1980s, the tools we now consider commonplace first began to make an impact: the personal computer, the mobile phone, the internet, digital photography and digital music. Communication was in the process of becoming simple, cheap and immediate.

> " Big Bang was a far-reaching programme of deregulation measures that opened up the City to foreign banks. "

Computing power went from being expensive and inaccessible to affordable, and from large mainframes sitting in computer labs to PCs sitting on everyone's desks. The individual immediately had the potential to become massively more productive. These technological developments were not slow to make their impact in the financial markets. In particular, the advent of the PC, and networks connecting them to servers, allowed a massive growth in derivatives as huge Monte-Carlo simulations could price and calculate the risk of thousands of new exotic financial products recorded in databases.

The traders' models could then convert the risks of those customised derivative products into approximate equivalent liquid plain vanilla bond positions and exchange-traded futures and options, allowing solid, quick and efficient risk management.

Nor were these changes limited to technology. In London, the freeing up of regulations and the unwinding of old taboos proceeded apace. A far-reaching

---

[13] Alan Greenspan, *The Age of Turbulence* (The Penguin Group, 2007), p. 52.

programme of deregulation measures known collectively as Big Bang was enacted in 1986, opening the once hallowed square mile to foreign banks. American, Japanese and European bankers arrived in such strength that the old boys' network that had ruled the City was diluted to the point of quasi-extinction. Where once a small group of men drawn from a cohesive social background might have run such institutions as Morgan Grenfell, now newcomers, including but not exclusively Germans and Americans, swiftly moved in.

Morgan Grenfell, the most blue-chip of venerable merchant banks, was bought by Deutsche Bank. Where it led, others followed. Warburgs fell to the Swiss, and Cazenove, the Queen's stockbroker, was bought by Chase Manhattan. Barings, the most aloof of them all, was brought to its knees by Nick Leeson in Asia, who bet the bank's money on a one-way trade against the Nikkei falling.[14] Barings would be absorbed by ING. Gradually, a job creation scheme for a select number of the English upper middle classes became radically widened as a recruiting spree for the rapidly expanding financial services gathered enormous momentum. Soon London became the hub of a vastly expanded business world which interlocked lawyers, consultants, accountants and bankers in one throbbing hive of activity.

> **As the City flourished the pressure on banks to increase their return on capital intensified.**

As this expansion gathered pace, two trends could be discerned. First, thanks to its unique position between the US and Asia, London's advantages as a financial centre grew exponentially. As the perception of this geographical advantage emerged, a talented indigenous workforce sprung up to fill many posts and form a nouveau-riche class. Second, as a result of the lack of a sufficiently large and well-educated UK white-collar workforce, foreigners flocked to work in the City of London. The City, together with the government itself, encouraged this immigration through a combination of light regulation and tax incentives for non-domiciled workers.

As the City flourished, the activities of the bankers also developed. The pressure on banks to increase their **return on capital** (ROC) intensified. Their decision-making became increasingly the province of the fiercely numerate,

---

[14] *Financial Times*, Review: 'Fall of the House of Baring', 3/3/1999.

and the phrases quant, financial engineer and turbo-capitalism were born. But this was not the full reality. With the end of the cold war and the triumph of the West over the corrupt and inefficient centralised economies of the Warsaw Pact, restraint and any sense of the state acting as a referee in the markets became less easy to uphold. It may have been necessary for capitalism to present a human face during the cold war in which ideologies were pitched against each other across the globe in a perpetual struggle for advantage, but the failure of communism and collapse of the Eastern bloc gave an added boost to the West and encouraged ever more inventive ways of deploying capital.

Conservatives on risk

Many conservatives had a great respect for all that they did not understand and for their inability to know exactly what forces were affecting the society they were leading. They had great respect for their inability to predict future events. Greenspan explained his thinking along these lines in a number of speeches. He said he believed the greatest change that had occurred during his time at the Fed was the development of monetary policy based not upon just a single best view of the future but on all of the possible futures and their probabilities of occurrence and relative costs or benefits. In a speech in July 2004 he said:

> The Federal Reserve's experiences over the past two decades make it clear that uncertainty is not just a pervasive feature of the monetary policy landscape; it is the defining characteristic of that landscape. The term 'uncertainty' is meant here to encompass both 'Knightian uncertainty', in which the probability distribution of outcomes is unknown, and 'risk' in which uncertainty of outcomes is delimited by a known probability distribution.

> Knightian uncertainty is by definition risk which cannot be measured. In real-world social systems, due to the inability to know what people will do and especially due to the self-referential nature of social systems such as markets, Knightian uncertainty is rampant. In practice, one is never quite sure what type of uncertainty one is dealing with in real time, and it may be best to think of a continuum ranging from well-defined risks to the truly unknown.[15]

---

[15] Remarks by Chairman Alan Greenspan at the Meetings of the American Economic Association, San Diego, California, 03/01/2004,
www.federalreserve.gov/BoardDocs/Speeches/2004/20040103/default.htm

This same respect for uncertainty and the inability to predetermine the future was clearly shared by conservative protagonists across the Republican administrations. Donald Rumsfeld, the irascible secretary of defense, well described a similar healthy respect for uncertainty during a press conference at NATO Headquarters in June 2002:

> There are things we know that we know. There are known unknowns. That is to say there are things that we now know we don't know. But there are also unknown unknowns. There are things we do not know we don't know. So when we do the best we can and we pull all this information together and we then say well that's basically what we see as the situation; that is really only the known knowns and the known unknowns. And each year we discover a few more of those unknown unknowns.

> There's another way to phrase that and that is that the absence of evidence is not evidence of absence. It is basically saying the same thing in a different way. Simply because you do not have evidence that something exists does not mean that you have evidence that it does not exist.[16]

Many criticise Rumsfeld for his strategic thinking but here we feel he was expressing an idea that is clearly legitimate.

Indeed not only conservative Republicans held these views. The Clinton Democrat administration harboured a similar approach to uncertainty. Robert Rubin, former star arbitrage trader and chairman of Goldman Sachs who became Treasury Secretary under Clinton, wrote in his memoirs, aptly titled *In an Uncertain World*:

> For me, probabilistic thinking has long been a highly conscious process. I imagine the mind as a virtual legal pad, with the factors involved in the decision gathered, weighed, and totalled up. To describe probabilistic thinking this way does not, however, mean that it can be reduced to a mathematical formula, with the best decision jumping automatically off a legal pad. Sound decisions are based on identifying relevant variables and attaching probabilities to them. That's an analytic process but also involves subjective judgments. The ultimate decision then reflects all of this input, but also instinct, experience and 'feel'... At the core of this outlook is the conviction

---

[16] www.defenselink.gov/transcripts/transcript.aspx?transcriptid=3490

that nothing can be proven to be certain... And once you enter the realm of probabilities, nothing is ever simple again.[17]

We are faced then with a Federal Reserve Chairman and multiple Presidential administrations that had a huge respect for at least two things: the massive productivity and innovation which could be released by reducing regulations, and the importance of uncertainty.

That was, of course, the platform for the 2007-2009 crisis.

The rise of the machines: new financial products

The unleashing of innovation meant a massive increase in new financial products which traded in huge volumes, and were managed by traders with newly built models that utilised microprocessors.

Interest rate and FX derivatives volumes expanded exponentially. This was followed by the same expansion in equity derivatives, commodity derivatives and later credit derivatives. There were attempts to slow and regulate this growth, but they were squashed as this innovation was seen to be adding great value to a growing economy. Banks were printing profits and increasing returns on capital like never before.

In early 1998 one official in the Clinton administration recognised a need for regulation of derivatives that went further than the self-regulation backed by banks, the Federal Reserve and the Treasury. Brooksley Born was the Chairperson of the US Commodity Futures Trading Commission (CFTC) and she saw numerous reasons for regulating over the counter (OTC) derivatives in the same way exchange-traded futures and options were. She proposed that closer regulation and transparency would be needed to prevent a major calamitous financial event from occurring. In comments to the CFTC in 1998 she said:

> **" The problem faced by LTCM and the reason they nearly created a systemic financial crisis was due to their excessively high leverage. "**

---

[17] Robert E. Rubin and Jacob Weisberg, *In an Uncertain World* (Random House, 2003), p. xi.

Reportedly, LTCM managed to borrow approximately 100 times its capital and to hold derivatives positions with a notional value of approximately $1.25 trillion or 1000 times its capital... This unlimited borrowing in the OTC derivatives market, like the unlimited borrowing on securities that contributed to the Great Depression, may pose grave dangers to our economy.[18]

The problem faced by LTCM and the reason they nearly created a systemic financial crisis was due to their excessively high leverage. It is the same leverage which contributed to the Great Depression. It is the same leverage which caused the 2007-2009 crisis and which continues to go unmeasured. None of the individual counterparts to LTCM were apparently aware of the extremely high levels of leverage they were taking on very low-risk securities. Very high leverage on accurately predicted positive return distributions means vast returns for investors and enormous wealth. However, very high leverage also means that even small errors in the price distributions of the assets aggregated by these financiers could cause enormous losses. Further, if the leverage is high enough then there can be systemic consequences.

The regulations proposed by the CFTC under Brooksley Born in 1998 were opposed by a lobbying effort on the part of derivatives and bond dealers. The main thrust of the lobbyists' argument was simple. Legal advisers had the opinion that regulation of OTC derivatives by the CFTC might call into question the legal validity of the contracts already outstanding. If the exemption was removed these contracts might be

> **Greenspan had huge respect for uncertainty but the need for unfettered development of financial products was considered more important than increasing regulation.**

considered illegal futures contracts and counterparts might call into question their legal viability. If some customers decided not to perform on that basis, chaos might break loose as no one would know their actual trading positions. The proposal was apparently rescinded by President Clinton's Working Group on Financial Markets. The OTC derivatives market remained free of Born's proposed new regulation.

---

[18] 'The lessons of Long-Term Capital Management, L.P.', Remarks of Brooksley Born, Chairperson, Commodity Futures Trading Commission, Chicago Kent-IIT Commodities Law Institute, Chicago, Illinois, 15 October 1998.

So while Greenspan and many members of multiple administrations had huge respect for uncertainty, the need for unfettered development of financial products was considered of greater import and value. What we will show through numerous examples is that the same levels of leverage evident in the 1998 crisis were replicated in the 21st century's shadow banking system, with AAA-rated credits, which required very little capital under Basel rules. This same excessive use of leverage can be pinpointed as being behind the cause, speed and severity of the 2007-2009 global banking crisis.

This is not to say that there weren't many warnings that the unfettered leverage and innovation of derivative products might create certain risks. There were many warnings through time that clearly indicated that 'true' leverage or sensitivity to errors in forecasted returns should be reported transparently and regulated.

The crash of 1929 and investment trusts

From reading *The Great Crash 1929* by John Kenneth Galbraith it becomes evident that there are many parallels between that financial calamity and the crisis of 2007-2009.

Firstly, in the late 1920s buying stock on margin was common and at times it was possible to put up just 10% margin against loans used to buy stocks. A margin of 10% meant that one could buy $100 of stock while putting up just $10 in capital. This by itself is a ten-times leveraged investment. As the equities purchased themselves will of course be leveraged investments, there is a layering of leverage and, as we will show later, the risk is multiplied.

Similarly, the financial markets of 1929 had their own version of the 21st century's *shadow banking system*, a term coined by Paul McCulley at the 2007 Kansas City Federal Reserve Bank's Jackson Hole Conference, which we will examine in greater detail later. In the 1920s this shadow system was made up of the investment trusts and holding companies. Investment trusts were vehicles originally set up to give smaller investors access to a more diversified investment portfolio. As time went on, however, investment trusts became investment vehicles which themselves issued debt, preferred shares and common equity, whose proceeds were then used to buy common equity. This approach facilitated leveraged investment in equities, much as the 21st century CDOs and SIVs we will examine later facilitated leveraged investments in debt securities.

How important was this?

According to Galbraith:

> In 1927 the trusts sold to the public about $400,000,000 worth of securities; in 1929 they marketed an estimated three billions' worth. This was at least a third of all new capital issues in that year; by the autumn of 1929 the total assets of the investment trusts were estimated to exceed eight billion dollars. They had increased approximately eleven-fold since the beginning of 1927.[19]

According to the US Department of Commerce's Bureau of Economic Analysis, US GDP was $103.6bn in 1929, and $14,258.7bn in 2009. Using GDP as a measure to understand the importance of $8bn of investment trusts in 1929, we see that it was 7.7% of GDP, or in today's terms the equivalent of $1.1 trillion. As we will see this is of similar magnitude to today's cash CDO market.

Investment trusts and holding companies were set up by professional managers promising enormous returns, and were often associated with major investment banks. Managers of the trusts might get paid based on the amount of assets outstanding, or on their returns. Leverage in some of these vehicles was layered several times. An investment trust could issue common stock and debt, and use those proceeds to buy the common stock of another investment trust, and so on. This was eerily similar to the CDOs and SIVs of the 21st century shadow banking system.

Much like an investment trust or holding company in the late 1920s might issue various tranches of securities in order to purchase the equity of other investment trusts or holding companies, who themselves had issued tranched securities to buy the equity in the common stocks of operating companies, the CDOs of the 2000s issued tranches of securities in order to buy the **mezzanine** tranches of CDOs and ABSs, those ABSs themselves having issued tranched securities in order to buy loans which had been issued to borrowers. In both the 1920s and 2000s then, similar vehicles were created – fuelling massive demand for equities in the 1920s, and massive demand for ABSs such as subprime mortgage-backed securities in the 2000s – resulting in leverage-driven bubbles which eventually burst.

---

[19] John Kenneth Galbraith, *The Great Crash 1929* (Houghton Mifflin Company, 1954), p. 50.

The Crash of 1987 and the dangers of leverage

In October 1987 the US stock market experienced its worst single day fall in its history. Afterwards, many blamed the extreme violence of that one day move on 'portfolio insurance'. Portfolio insurance represented a risk very similar to a set of out of the money equity put options. We will show later how CDOs, and especially super senior tranches of **structured finance CDOs**, also have risks similar to massive out-of-the-money options.[20] Many fund managers had signed up for the algorithmic strategy of portfolio insurance to hedge their fund positions. This is best described by Richard Bookstaber in his book *A Demon of Our Own Design*. Bookstaber was managing the portfolio insurance business for Morgan Stanley on the day of the crash. He says:

> The 1987 crash simply was not the result of rational reaction to new information. What sort of information could have led the market to drop more than 20 percent on October 19th and jump 12 percent early the next morning, only to fall 10 percent in the following few hours. Nor was it a matter of herd psychology. The moon and stars did not align to lead broad segments of the market to wake up Monday morning and decide to dump their shares. In fact, a select and concentrated set of firms generated the selling demand on the 16th and the 19th.[21]

" Warnings that product innovation was leading to massive leverage went unheeded and self-regulation by banks won the day. "

The crash of 1987 was caused by the excessive selling which was required by portfolio insurance, and no one had foreseen what the consequences of the widespread use of this product would be when everyone tried to de-lever at once. Portfolio insurance forced selling, which lowered prices, which then forced more selling. The simple existence of the very high volume of portfolio insurance increased the risk of its own algorithm being triggered.

Greenspan responded with the primary tool he would use for the entirety of his reign as Chairman of the Federal Reserve: monetary policy. Greenspan

---

[20] Out of the money options are those whose strike prices yield no intrinsic value given current market prices of the underlying. For example, a put option to sell stock ABC struck at $80 is out of the money if the price of ABC stock is $100.

[21] Richard Bookstaber, *A Demon of Our Own Design* (John Wiley and Sons, 2007), p. 14.

wisely understood that the crash might have a significant negative impact on economic activity and he lowered rates immediately.

There followed many further warnings to the effect that product innovation was leading to massive leverage, but all those calls went unheeded in terms of response by regulators to reign in leverage. Self-regulation by the banks for their own accounts and for the protection of their customers won the day (or actually decades).

The Japanese financial crisis

Meanwhile, from 1985 to late 1989, the Nikkei stock index soared from 11,588 to 38,916; 336% in less than five years. During the run, real estate prices also rose dramatically. Subsequently, the Nikkei collapsed to below 8000 and as of early 2010 remained well below its 1989 peak. The Japanese banking system came under enormous pressure and required multiple bailouts, much as US and European banks required bailouts during the 2007-2009 crisis.

Much like the investment trusts of the 1920s and the shadow banking system of the 2000s, the Japanese financial system had a structure whereby leverage, and therefore risk, was multiplied.

The Japanese financial system was characterised by enormous cross shareholdings and outright ownership of equity shares by corporations. Japanese banks owned shares of Japanese insurance companies, while those same Japanese insurance companies might have held shares or subordinated debt in those same banks. When we follow our new language of risk later on in the book, we will see that this causes an infinite loop in the multiplication of risk. This Japanese banking risk was very similar to the risks which were evident in the period leading up to the 2007-2009 crisis in some SIVs whereby banks owned the income notes of SIVs, who themselves owned the subordinated debt of financial institutions, thus multiplying risk. When this practice is expanded on a large scale, it creates systemic risk.

Further, according to Mark Scher, 1985 to 1990 in Japan "was a period of intensive *zaitech* (financial engineering) investment in securities by corporations, unrelated to investment for cross-shareholding purposes."[22] This

---

[22] Mark Scher, 'Bank-firm Cross-shareholding in Japan: What is it, why does it matter, is it winding down?', DESA Discussion Paper No. 15, February 2001.

purchase of leveraged securities, namely equities, by leveraged corporations assisted the Nikkei's incredible rally and helped to instigate its subsequent fall, much as the financial engineering of the 2000s saw special purpose companies buy the mezzanine debt of special purpose companies, which bought the mezzanine debt of subprime mortgage-backed securities, facilitating soaring housing prices in the US. This is also similar to the way in which investment trusts of the 1920s bought the shares of investment trusts, who bought common equities, fuelling the initial rally and subsequent bust of stock prices in 1929.

> **" Much like the investment trusts of the 1920s and the shadow banking system of the 2000s, the Japanese financial system had a structure whereby leverage and risk were multiplied. "**

How important were bank shareholdings in Japan? The run up of share prices was directly supported by bank and insurance company purchases as financial institutions increased their holdings from around 10% of all shares listed on the Tokyo Stock Exchange in 1950, to a peak of over 40% in 1989, after which their percentage holdings declined.[23] According to Kazuo Ueda, "Large Japanese banks had capital ratios barely above 8% at the start of the 1990s, with about half of the 8% accounted for by unrealised capital gains on their equity positions."[24]

Half of the regulatory equity capital of Japanese banks was made up of their holdings of equity in other companies, and of these holdings many were in other financial institutions. Meanwhile many banking regulators would require that equity shareholdings be deducted from capital.

The Basel Committee on Banking Supervision was very concerned about this type of risk when they issued their original capital standards in 1988. They stated: "The committee is very conscious that such double gearing (or 'double leveraging') can have systemic dangers for the banking system by making it more vulnerable to the rapid transmission of problems from one institution to another and some members consider these dangers justify a full deduction of such holdings."[25] None the less, the Basel committee missed the leverage which

---

[23] Ibid.

[24] Kazuo Ueda, BIS working paper, 'The Japanese banking crisis in the 1990s', 12/12/2005, www.bis.org/publ/plcy07q.pdf

[25] Basel Committee on Banking Supervision, 'International Convergence of Capital Measurement and Capital Standards', Basel, July 1988, www.bis.org/publ/bcbs04a.pdf

was building in the system, and as we will see it did not make specific rules to regulate its growth.

Further financial crises

On 4 February 1994, the Federal Reserve raised interest rates for the first time in almost five years in response to a full recovery of the US economy from the 1991 recession. This rise in rates had a dramatic effect on those who had levered positions in interest rate derivatives and mortgage-backed securities markets, and who had grown accustomed to the low steady rates which had prevailed for some time. David Askin's mortgage-backed hedge fund, due to its high leverage, was the first victim. According to a *New York Times* article of April 1994:

> In the last two months, the $600 million that Askin had managed for wealthy individuals and institutions has essentially been wiped out.
>
> Askin's funds borrowed another $1.4 billion from brokerage firms, so at their peak the funds controlled about $2 billion of complex and rarely traded bonds backed by home mortgages. As interest rates rose, the price of those bonds fell sharply.
>
> The funds managed by Askin were Granite Partners, the Granite Corporation and Quartz Hedge Fund. The two Granite funds used a strategy known as 'market neutral,' which called for buying combinations of exotic mortgage-backed securities in such a way that they would not gain or lose money, in theory, as a result of interest rate changes. In the face of a very rapid rise in rates and a decline in demand for the mortgage-backed securities, Askin's strategy did not work and the funds lost value quickly.[26]

The fund had exposures to exotic mortgage-backed securities, and the funds presumably had highly tuned models which seemingly implied little or no risk. The fund was intended as 'market neutral'. Nonetheless, the leverage they used in combination with the complexity of their mortgage positions seemingly blew up, much as did the AAA-rated subprime mortgages of the recent credit crisis.

Askin would not be the only victim though. Orange County California had taken on levered bets in US Treasury bonds and in levered derivatives. These made money in a low and falling rate environment, but due to their leverage

---

[26] *New York Times*, 08/04/2004.

would blow up in a rising rate environment. Indeed, Orange County lost so much that it needed to declare bankruptcy.

The Fed responded strongly. They immediately called the CEOs of all of the major New York banks and informed them that they had better understand the risks in these instruments, had better ensure that they were comfortable with their sales practices and that clients were only sold products which were appropriate.

The Long-Term Capital Management crisis

In 1997 there was the Asian crisis. In 1998, we had the Russian and LTCM crises. The LTCM crisis hit at the heart of the derivatives and financial engineering community as the company was considered the best and the brightest; among its employees were two Nobel Laureates – in Robert C. Merton and Myron Scholes – and David Wiley Mullins Jr., a former vice-chairman at the Federal Reserve.[27] Nonetheless, LTCM was caught out on a very basic point: the markets were behaving in a way which was not predicted by history or by the models they were using. The excessive leverage used by the fund brought them to the verge of bankruptcy and the financial system to the verge of collapse. In response, the Fed called in the heads of the banks which were lenders and counterparts to LTCM in order to ensure that they cleaned up their mess. The banks agreed to short-term credit lines in order to shore up LTCM and give it enough time to unwind its trades in an orderly fashion. The one bank which refused to play ball would be the first to bite the dust in the 2007-2009 crisis – Bear Stearns.

In the epilogue of *When Genius Failed*, Roger Lowenstein summarises the lessons learned from the LTCM crisis. As we will see throughout this book, these are important themes that were repeated in the 2007-2009 crisis.

According to Lowenstein:

> The investor who is highly leveraged and illiquid is playing Russian roulette. Uncertainty as opposed to risk, is an indefinite condition, one that does not conform to numerical straitjackets.

> The belief that tomorrow's risks can be inferred from yesterday's prices and volatilities prevails at virtually every investment bank and trading desk. This was Long-Term's biggest mistake, and its stunning

---

[27] The models of Robert C. Merton would become the basis for much of the Basel II capital rules.

losses betrayed the flaw in the very heart – the very brain – of modern finance.[28]

In a damning statement, Lowenstein goes on to say:

> The next time Merton proposes an elegant model to manage risks and foretell odds, the next time a computer with a perfect memory of the past is said to quantify the risks of the future, investors should run – and quickly – the other way.[29]

Later, in 2005, the Basel Committee on Banking Supervision paper 'An Explanatory note on the Basel II IRB Risk Weight Functions' refered to Merton, his models and papers no fewer than ten times, as the basis of its approach to minimum regulatory capital requirements.

In response to the 1997 and 1998 crises, and due to their potential and unknowable negative impact on the US economy, Greenspan lowered rates, in each case dramatically. At the same time, by 1999 the unfettered capitalism and supportive monetary policy had helped to create an environment of incredible innovation.

" LTCM was caught out on a very basic point: the markets were behaving in a way which was not predicted by history or by the models they were using. "

In late 1999, even though it was clear that the US economy was growing too fast, Greenspan kept rates low due to the uncertainty around the turn of the millennium and the feared impact on computer systems. As it turned out, the millennium passed smoothly with no systemic computer glitches and monetary policy had unnecessarily been kept loose. As that risk passed Greenspan raised rates dramatically and the stock bubble, which had been created by a real set of innovations combined with easy policy and irrational exuberance, came to an end.

---

[28] Roger Lowenstein, *When Genius Failed* (Random House, 2000), pp. 234-235.

[29] Ibid., p. 235.

Shadow banking

As the stock market cratered and the economy weakened, Greenspan saw the balance of risks in the US economy as being weighted more heavily towards weakness and lowered rates dramatically. This new drop in rates had its intended consequence: the first and most powerful force in the monetary policy transmission mechanism is to increase demand for interest-rate sensitive purchases. With the unquenchable appetite for new debt created by the shadow banking system, based upon its recently innovated structures, auto sales and new home sales

> **" The shadow banking system created an unquenchable appetite for new debt which fuelled the housing bubble and became the major force in creating unregulated leverage. "**

soared. The home became the ATM for unending consumption. The shadow banking system became the major new force in creating leverage, which was completely unregulated, across the global banking system.

Ironically, those who appeared to have an unquenchable appetite for this consumerism would be those who would suffer most in the fallout. They were those who were most politically aware and had traditionally formed the backbone of the struggle of democracies against totalitarianism: the middle classes. Free markets in banking and investment led to an excessive increase in both the scale and complexity of borrowing. As these became more international, they could not be restrained by regulation as governments which pursued national regulation were soon outflanked by other jurisdictions.

At the same time, unrelated to the developments in banking, internationalisation of the economy led many middle-class salaries to stagnate, and higher living standards were made sustainable only by spending funds raised against assets, particularly housing. Thus the bankers were first and foremost meeting a need. While the rapid expansion of debt inflated the price of homes, increased consumerism was possible, but the pressure building up was ominous

In order to increase profits, building societies de-mutualised and became listed entities. Banks, which previously had made a solid profit on lending and other low-octane activities, were forced to enter markets where profits could be maintained. The structures used to achieve this were flawed, but the bankers were largely ignorant of this. This in particular applied to leverage that went unmeasured and proved to be more responsible than anything else for a catastrophic mispricing of risk.

Even in Germany, a country renowned for caution in banking matters and with a solid middle class, banks came under increasing pressure to increase their return on capital. By 2003, collateralised debt obligation issuance was in full flood, encouraged not least by the banks' scramble to increase ROC. As long as the painstaking documentation work with the rating agencies was done, nearly anything could be securitised, structured and sold on.

Rating agencies

The rating agencies, anxious to play a role in a market which needed good third-party risk analysis, fed the enthusiasm. What the public may have regarded as objective, independent arbiters of risk were also – it should not be forgotten – high-margin businesses. Between 2003 and 2006, Moody's doubled its revenue and more than tripled its stock price. Their main customers, however, were the banks and investment houses who relied on the CDO ratings (which were often the outcome of a prolonged negotiation).

> **"The rating agencies, anxious to play a role in a market which needed good third-party risk analysis, fed the enthusiasm. "**

The agencies affixed their seal of approval to countless securities now so unloved that they are commonly described as toxic. They were, in turn, paid by the corporations whose debt they were rating, earning billions of dollars in fees. This did not go unnoticed – some important figures did comment on what was happening. For example, in his 2009 Berkshire Hathaway letter Warren Buffett urged investors to pose tough questions of the rating agencies.

The agencies, however, did publish many methodology papers outlining their approach to ratings, trying to make them as transparent as possible. It is also important to recognise that the big story here is one of leverage which went unmeasured and the finger should not be pointed solely at the rating agencies.

The failure to measure leverage

Eleven companies, which have either failed or were bailed out by the US government in late 2008 and early 2009, collapsed with investment-grade ratings as if as the *New York Times* observed, they were "deathly ill patients being given clean bills of health". But because of the failure to measure leverage, the doctors were measuring the wrong thing: the patient's blood thickness, not their heartbeat. The rating agencies appear to have been naïve about the risks they were facilitating.

Frank Partnoy, professor at the University of San Diego, noted: "Imagine if you had a rabbi who said all the laws of kosher depend on whether this rabbi decides if food is kosher or not. If the rules say you have to use this rabbi he could be totally wrong but it won't affect the value of his franchise." As Partnoy pointed out, "A lot of investors have been eating pork these past three decades."[30]

But it was a collective conceptual error which caused this. As Warren Buffett noted: "Indeed the stupefying losses in mortgage-related securities came in large part because of flawed history-based models used by salesmen, rating agencies and investors."[31]

This book will show that these flawed models can be replaced by a paradigm shift in how risk is assessed and that the key to that shift is the measurement of leverage. If we can rectify these conceptual errors, we will be more than halfway down the road to restoring confidence.

> **In June 2008 the figure of asset-backed securities outstanding in the US was $2498 bn.**

Massive increases in lending were, for the reasons outlined above, welcomed by many. But the numbers which characterised the increase are truly stupendous. According to the Securities Industry and Financial Markets Association (SIFMA), US **asset-backed securities** (ABS) outstanding in 1990 were only US$100 billion. By the end of 2000, the figure was US$900 billion, and by June 2008 it had risen to US$2498 billion. This represents a 19.5% annualised growth rate for eighteen years.[32]

By 2007 more than half of all the money borrowed in US credit markets was done via ABS or securitisation. How could there have been such a large increase in lending via securitisation? Where in particular did all the required capital come from? Was there a massive increase in capital seeking risk, or

---

[30] David Segal, 'Buffet Is Unusually Silent on Rating Agencies', *New York Times*, 17/03/2009.

[31] David Segal, 'In Letter, Warren Buffet Concedes a Tough Year', *New York Times*, 28/02/2009.

[32] www.sifma.org

something else? There was, in fact, an enormous increase in leverage. How did this occur? Essentially regulators and market participants stopped measuring leverage.

So what is leverage and why is it important?

Leverage: hero or zero?

Leverage can be defined as capital plus borrowed funds, divided by the amount of capital only. Some call it gearing. Some call it investing on margin. Whatever it is named, it is of key importance to returns on investment.

For example, assume you have US$10 in capital and borrow an additional US$90. Your leverage is ($10 + $90)/$10, which is ten times. What does this mean for investment returns? Assume that you take the $100 you now have and invest it in securities for one year. Assume your borrowing cost is 5% (and for simplicity so is your cost of capital) and that your investments return 6%. Then your return net of your funding and cost of capital is 1% on your total assets, or $1. While 1% return on assets (ROA) may not seem impressive, it represents a 10% return on capital (ROC) – which is very impressive. The leverage takes a poor return on assets and converts it into a high return on capital.

> **Leverage takes a poor return on assets and converts it into a high return on capital.**

Now, if you run a company, bank, hedge fund or any investment vehicle, one focus will clearly be on ROC. Assuming your low 1% ROA is due to the fact that the assets purchased have a very low risk profile, or have very little variation in return over time, you can be confident that you will be able to maintain this ROC indefinitely.

The impact of Greenspan's monetary policies

The era during which Greenspan ran the Fed is sometimes called the 'great moderation', describing the falling volatility in economic output. This is well deserved for the finely tuned monetary policy which supported the US economy, but it misses something else that was happening.

The Federal Reserve's monetary policy has the objectives of supporting maximum sustainable employment, stable prices and moderate long-term interest rates. The Federal Open Market Committee (FOMC) is responsible for setting monetary policy for the Federal Reserve. Their main policy tool up until the credit crunch had been setting the Federal Funds rate.

In 1993, John Taylor insightfully published a paper describing a linear model which took two variables that represented the first two of the Fed's monetary policy objectives (actual vs. potential growth and actual vs. target inflation) as inputs, and whose output was a projected Fed funds target. It turned out that this did a very good job of describing what the Fed had done. Certain variations on this model – using actual vs. potential employment or the actual unemployment rate vs. the **non-accelerating inflation rate of unemployment** (NAIRU) – did even better. The Fed was clearly focused on its goals and the unemployment rate and the rate of inflation both reduced in volatility, and neared their optimal levels. A great moderation in terms of monetary policy goals was achieved.

By achieving this great moderation, the volatility in real GDP fell, and capacity utilisation rates remained high and stable. This meant that the variation in company and household cash flows was lower than it had been previously, which in general meant varying cash flows were having a less negative impact on ability to pay back debts. This in turn meant better predictability of ability to pay, and better ability to pay means fewer defaults, and better and more stable bond returns.

Investors with increasing confidence in returns

If an investor has high confidence in the distribution of future returns of his portfolio, it might look like this:

Assume again that this investor is ten times levered with $10 in capital and $90 borrowed. Say he takes his $100, invests it in ten bonds and his average return is 6%, again vs. cost of funds of 5%. Let's say that average return includes a return of negative 10% once in 100 years. A negative 10% ROA will mean the investor is wiped out. An investor might think that is an acceptable level of risk. On the other hand, what if the additional stability caused by the great moderation leads the investor to change their probability distribution of that great disaster (i.e. negative 10% ROA) and they now think the worst event in any 100-year period is halved to a negative 5%. In that case they will not be wiped out in any century according to their return expectations. What should they do then? If they are willing to risk a complete wipe out once every 100 years and their objective is to maximise ROC, then they should increase leverage.

Given the investor's assumption is that they will only get wiped out once every 100 years if they increase leverage to 20 times, they go ahead and do that. The investor then borrows $190 against their US$10 in capital; if the net ROA is again expected to be 1%, now the investor makes 20% ROC – a tremendous return.

What if the investor is highly regulated like a bank and wishes to increase leverage?

> **"** If an investor has high confidence in the distribution of future returns of his portfolio, he can increase leverage. **"**

Bankers have teams of people who serve internally and externally to build products which meet both the objectives of their client investors and the rules of their regulators. Via securitisation, derivatives and structuring, it is often possible to increase leverage while not, for example, increasing minimum required capital. This is mainly due to the fact that under Basel rules, regulators stopped measuring leverage. This is the heart of the cause of the credit crisis.

Companies, investment managers and banks strive to maximise ROC

Very simply, the owners of a bank or company expect the managers of that firm to achieve the highest possible ROC. If a company, hedge fund or bank achieves a low ROC relative to its competitors, its stock will underperform and its management will be put under enormous pressure. Investors are never pleased if their neighbour owns a company or invests in a fund with higher ROC.

It is very possible, of course, that two different managers may have very different predictions of the future return distributions. That being said, consider two managers who both have the same risk appetite as their investors – that is, that they should be willing to accept a once-in-a-century wipe out. If one manager thinks the worst once-in-a-century return is a negative 5% and the other a negative 10%, we can expect the former to have double the leverage of the latter. The manager with double the leverage will double the returns of the other manager as long as the returns are positive.

Of course, the opposite is also true. For example, if a negative 5% return occurs in the second year the manager has been in charge, and he was levered 20 times, he will then be wiped out and the game will be over. He will have failed and is unlikely to be backed by investors again. The conservative manager, on the other hand, will keep his job, and his investors will be very pleased with their superior returns.

Leverage is a dual edged sword used by both borrowers and banks. The higher the leverage the higher the potential returns both in the case of the borrower and in the case of the bank. The higher the leverage, the higher the risk of default of both the borrower and the bank. As we will show later, the 2007-2009 crisis was the outcome of high leverage used by subprime mortgage borrowers and by the financial institutions which facilitated their loans.

Basel II guidelines on risk

We will go into more detail in describing bank capital requirements in the following chapters, but a few words here will make a good point. Basel II required that banks be expected to be able to survive in any given year with a 99.9% confidence level. In practice, this is the same as saying that they should only be expected to be wiped out once every thousand years and need to aim for that level of risk appetite.

> **" The 2007-2009 crisis was the outcome of high leverage used by subprime mortgage borrowers and by the financial institutions which facilitated their loans. "**

Imagine what they are being asked to do: to predict with certainty what a once-in-1000-year flood would look like and manage to that. If you think about it, and if you subscribe to Alan Greenspan's, Robert Rubin's, Donald Rumsfeld's and Nassim Taleb's points of view, this is a Herculean task. Actually the ability to predict the return distribution to that level of accuracy is, in our view, quite impossible. The only way to be really confident would be to take no risk. Alternatively, one could be more aggressive and have higher returns on capital for 50 years and never be hit by a once-in-100-year storm and no one would ever know, of course, whether the manager had managed risk to a once-in-100-year or a once-in-a-1000-year wipe out. The career would be over long before anyone would know.

The Federal Reserve and stability of the financial system

An additional objective of the Federal Reserve is to ensure the stability of the financial system. Clearly, the great moderation in itself led to financial stability as cash flows became more stable and predictable for corporations and households. In addition, the Fed's quick reaction to crises with lower rates acted as a shock absorber, thus reducing the worst-case scenarios. But, as one can imagine, if the increased stability convinced managers that in order to manage to the same level of risk appetite they needed to increase leverage, the sensitivity to an error in the manager's projections of loss distributions would increase dramatically. The Fed, of course, has the ability to regulate leverage, and therefore limit this risk in that manner. In fact, central banks globally work together to align international standards of safety for banks so that all banks are kept to at least a minimum level of safety, under the guise of the Basel Committee.

Evidently, however, those regulations were flawed and as yet we have not seen any clear move to capture the unique risks in the system accurately enough to restore confidence. Of course, the main purpose of this book is to offer a new alternative measure which improves upon any of those in use at the time of writing.

New products developed over the 20-year period between the introduction of Basel I and II, in conjunction with these accords, transformed the required capital for lending to a fraction of what it once was. At the same time, the confidence investors and regulators placed in ratings was, as we will show, a fundamental conceptual error, for the ratings were in a large part dependent on subordination and therefore predicted loss distributions based on an unreliable history.

The rating agency models, in combination with the regulatory regime of Basel I and Basel II, encouraged a huge increase in leverage across the global financial system. This new level of leverage, achieved via new products and facilitated by banking regulations, is often called the shadow banking system. What were in fact conceptual errors became articles of faith for banks. These errors might have been avoided but we should not forget that those responsible for Basel I and II were dealing with new products that they had never seen before.

❝ As yet we have not seen any clear move to capture the unique risks in the system accurately enough to restore confidence. ❞

Though it is convenient, and no doubt will become an oft-repeated mantra, to think that all our woes are the result of moral hazard, the element of conceptual error was the fundamental cause of the 2007-2009 crisis. As we will show, the emphasis on **risk-weighted assets** (RWAs) allowed the measurement of leverage to be neglected.

Let us now turn to Basel I and II and examine in some detail how we got into this predicament before explaining the clear route out of it.

2

The Unintended Consequences Of Basel I And Basel II

"I can't believe that!" said Alice.

"Can't you?" the Queen said in a pitying tone. "Try again: draw a long breath, and shut your eyes." Alice laughed. "There's no use trying," she said: "one can't believe impossible things."

"I daresay you haven't had much practice," said the Queen. "When I was your age, I always did it for half-an-hour a day. Why, sometimes I've believed as many as six impossible things before breakfast."

From Lewis Carroll's *Through the Looking Glass,* Chapter 5

Chapter summary

This chapter will examine the unintended consequences of Basel I, Basel II and the 1996 Market Risk Amendment: the increase in systemic risk and the creation of the shadow banking system.

- Basel regulations laid the foundation for the establishment of the shadow banking system and for a massive increase in leverage which went unmeasured.

- By requiring no capital for undrawn committed facilities less than one year in maturity, Basel regulations fostered the birth of the ABCP conduit and the SIV.

- Basel I increased systemic risk by having lower bank capital requirements for owning other bank's liabilities than for other non-bank assets.

- The 1996 Market Risk Amendment facilitated the hiding of certain risks through Gaussian lenses, ignoring the effects of extreme – or fat tail – events.

- Basel II introduced ratings as a risk sensitive measure to determine required capital, which in combination with rating agency use of less than perfect correlation between default events facilitated a massive increase in leverage and systemic risk.

Basel I

The original Basel I accord was known as the Basel Capital Accord. It was well defined in a paper issued in July 1988 called 'International Convergence of Capital Measurement and Capital Standards'.

This accord defined a new measurement term: risk weighted assets (RWAs). In essence, assets that were deemed less risky required less capital. Assets considered riskier would require more capital. The bankers that met in Basel were not there to create anything that was too complex or sophisticated. The accord would have to be supported by all participants and, just as at any diplomatic summit, different points of view would have to be reconciled. In particular, the need to carry the accord across all of the G10 supervisory authorities meant that things would have to be kept simple.

As banks historically had been levered on the order of 12 or so times, the amount of capital required would be determined by dividing the risk weighted assets by 12.5. It was a very simple accord and it needed to be in order to get agreement. Even more so, given that the aim was to have it adopted by all banking regulators globally, implementation costs would need to be low.

This is not to underestimate the progress made here: as banks became more global, and as prudential capital requirements were generally driven by one's home regulator, Basel I promoted the creation of a more level playing field for banks in which to compete. If a bank in one jurisdiction could hold less capital against given risk, it would have a competitive advantage in attracting capital as it could achieve a higher return on capital for a given risk. A lower required capital amount would also mean that one could charge less to borrower clients while achieving the same return on capital. These potential distortions would, in theory, be ironed out by the accord.

Nevertheless, there would be a price to pay for this. A single standard meant a single optimal approach to banking; which ironically would mean a far less robust global banking system. Nature and Darwin have taught us that both diversity and adaptability are key to the survival of any species, and yet the implementation of an international capital standard in practice effected the elimination of diversity.

While the minimum capital standard of Basel I assured a minimum level of safety, it also had the unintended consequence of creating a lowest common denominator in terms of safety for banks in a rapidly globalising competitive banking environment. This lowest common denominator was outlined in the

1998 update of that 1988 accord. Table 2.1 shows how this increases the chance for systemic risk.

Table 2.1: Risk weights by category of on-balance-sheet asset

Risk weight	Category
0%	(a) Cash (b) Claims on central governments and central banks denominated in national currency and funded in that country (c) Other claims on OECD central governments and central banks (d) Claims collateralised by cash of OECD central-government securities or guaranteed by OECD central governments
0,10,20 or 50% (at national discretion)	(a) Claims on domestic public-sector entities, excluding central government, and loans guaranteed by or collateralised by securities issued by such entities
20%	(a) Claims on multilateral development banks (IBRD, IADB, AsDB, AfDB, EIB, EBRD) and claims guaranteed by, or collateralised by securities issued by such banks (b) Claims on banks incorporated in the OECD and claims guaranteed by OECD incorporated banks (c) Claims on securities firms incorporated in the OECD subject to comparable supervisory and regulatory arrangements, including in particular risk-based capital requirements, and claims guaranteed by these securities firms
100%	(a) Claims on the private sector (b) Claims on banks incorporated outside the OECD with a residual maturity of over one year

Source: 'Basel Committee: International convergence of capital measurement and capital standards', (July 1988, updated to April 1998), Annex 2, p. 17, www.bis.org/publ/bcbsc111.htm

Applying the risk-weight measurement rules, if you are a bank based within a country that is a member of the Organisation for Economic Co-operation and Development (OECD) and you lend to another bank which is also a member of the OECD, this asset receives a 20% risk weight. On the other hand, if you lend to other entities which are not a member of the club, those assets get a 100% risk weight.

This asymmetry is significant.

In other words, lending within the club of banks gets a preferential capital treatment. Under these rules you only need 20% times 8%, or 1.6%, capital allocated for any loan to any OECD bank. You therefore get to lend to highly levered institutions at a preferential capital requirement simply because they are members of the club.

This preferential treatment had further consequences: it fostered increased trading and lending among banks, and therefore made them more interconnected.

It is easy to extrapolate from this a domino effect – if any member of the club were to become weakened by defaults, that injury would fall increasingly on the shoulders of other members. This inevitably would mean an increase in systemic risk. If Merrill Lynch or Banque AIG were to go bust it is likely they would take many more members with them, and potentially even the entire financial system.

> **"Basel I increased lending among banks, which made them more interconnected, and augmented systemic risk. 🟥🟥**

Conversely, the opposite approach would create a far more robust system. For example, if it were detrimental in terms of required capital to lend between members of the club then the likelihood of one member being weakened by the weakness or default of another member would fall dramatically. Higher capital requirements on interbank risk would reduce systemic risk.

Safe vs. dangerous collateral agreements

Similarly the consistent use of collateral agreements between bank counterparts for trading risks such as derivatives acts as a buffer in reducing systemic risks. One lesson learned from the crisis appears to be that the mark-to-markets used for daily collateral movements for margin requirements actually worked quite well between banks. Likewise, exchange-driven trading with similar daily margin requirements acted well as a good systemic buffer.

On the other hand, collateral agreements which required collateral only in the case of the significant downgrade of one party added to systemic risks. If a party was downgraded because of losses on assets on which the party also had collateral agreements triggered by downgrades, a self-feeding downward spiral might occur. The falling asset prices cause a downgrade which then causes a collateral call. This collateral call may force selling of those assets which then causes yet further losses. Financial institutions with robust daily collateral agreements between them likely pose a far less systemic threat than those with either no collateral agreements between them, or those with collateral agreements which are triggered only by downgrades.

The negative consequences of Basel I

Basel I also had other effects which were to have not entirely beneficial consequences. As there was no differentiation in capital requirements for highly rated assets versus non-investment-grade assets, there would be some temptation to increase risk by focusing on lending to lesser-rated credits.

Alternatively, there would be a desire to try to get more highly-rated credits that a bank felt were good lending risks off the balance sheet.

But this was not all. Far more dramatic than the above increase in systemic risk caused by Basel I was the accord's handling of credit conversion factors for off-balance-sheet items.

In particular, item eight from the list in the capital accord would lead directly to the birth of the shadow banking system:

Items 7 and 8 from the Basel I Capital Accord

7.   Other commitments (e.g. formal standby facilities and credit lines) with original maturity over one year – 50%.

8.   Similar commitments with an original maturity of up to one year, or which can be unconditionally cancelled at any time – 0%.

Risks falling under category eight were relegated to a 0% risk weight.

Essentially, this would allow undrawn committed credit facilities to off-balance-sheet vehicles to be written by banks with absolutely no regulatory capital requirement. These vehicles would become the much written about conduits and SIVs (special investment vehicles) of the shadow banking system.

The liquidity facility capital requirement would be zero: no capital required.

While the undrawn committed facilities themselves may not have yielded enormous income, they facilitated the ability of banks to fund assets off-balance-sheet and to earn the margin between the cost of funding and the income from the assets, which could be large.[33] In chapter three we will explore these structures in much greater depth.

Increasing leverage means increasing returns on capital (ROC) and the ability to lower prices on lending. No capital required means one could theoretically become infinitely leveraged and therefore achieve an infinite return on capital. The Basel I Accord did not address this issue. On the contrary, it hid the risk of undrawn committed facilities and, in our view, helped to create the foundation for the credit crisis.

> " Basel I did not differentiate the capital required for AAA-rated assets from the capital required for lower rated or more highly levered assets. "

The accord was a compromise between different governments and the result was that perhaps more value was placed on reaching an agreement than thinking through all the consequences. The accord was too simple. By not differentiating the capital required for AAA-rated assets – the less levered or less risky assets – from that required of non-investment grade or more highly levered assets, bankers were given more reason to use conduits which were supported by undrawn committed facilities maturing in less than one year. These vehicles would be highly rated and funded by issuing **asset-backed commercial paper (ABCP)** to money market funds.

These developments also led to the introduction by banks of securitised portfolios of corporate loans, as there was seemingly little guidance on handling the capital requirements for tranches of such structures.

This lack of differentiation of capital requirements between less vs. more risky securities was a flaw which Basel II attempted to address, though incompletely. We discuss this in further depth below.

Another flaw in Basel I that should be noted is that it did not differentiate between assets which were in trading books and those which were in banking books; though this would in part be addressed by the 1996 Market Risk Amendment.

---

[33] Under Basel II this rule has been revised considerably.

The 1996 Market Risk Amendment: hiding risks using Gaussian lenses

The intent of this amendment was to "provide an explicit capital cushion for price risks to which banks are exposed, particularly those arising from their trading activities."[34]

Again, while this may have seemed as if it would lead to a more robust banking system as more risks were being measured and brought under a harmonised system of regulations, it in fact had the opposite effect. The amendment allowed banking institutions to use flawed internal models for supervisory capital requirements for market risks.

The amendment reaffirmed "the appropriateness of requiring banks to calculate VaR based on the instantaneous shock equivalent of a 10-day move in prices (the holding period)." **Value at risk** or VaR measures variation of the history of prices for a given market and assumes that the underlying distribution is **Gaussian** or thin-tailed.[35]

By a thin-tailed distribution we mean one whereby not only are outlier events unlikely, but they are also reasonably predictable. For example, imagine the distribution of heights of adults; whose average might be, say, 5'5". If we survey the heights of 100,000 widely different adults we will likely start to get a very good idea of the distribution of all adult heights. The height of the tallest man on record, according to Guinness World Records, is 8'11". While this is amazing, it is much less than two times the average and not beyond one's reasonable imagination. By adding the tallest human being on record to our 100,000 survey participants the average changes by six one-thousandths of one inch; quite a small change. The average remains around 5'5".

Price distributions of actual markets, on the other hand, are wild and unpredictable. Markets are social phenomena with feedback mechanisms and are very fat-tailed. For an example of a fat-tailed distribution due to social phenomena, assume now instead of surveying adult heights we survey average wealth in the United States. If we survey 100,000 people it is easy to imagine we could get an average wealth of, say, $80,000. Now compare this to what the richest man in America might be worth, say $40 billion. This individual

---

[34] 'Overview of the Amendment to the Capital Accord to Incorporate Market Risks', Basel Committee on Banking Supervision, January, 1996, www.bis.org/publ/bcbs23.pdf

[35] Gaussian distributions are also known as normal or bell-shaped distributions.

would be worth 500,000 times the average. When we take a new average which includes this one additional data point, we get $480,000, or six times the original average. Nowhere in our survey did we ever get any inclination that this new data point might be possible. The richest person's wealth is totally unexpected and unpredictable.

The same phenomenon is true of market price changes. According to Benoit Mandelbrot, who for more than 40 years has been warning of the error in using Gaussian distributions to model market movements: "The data overwhelmingly show that the magnitude of price changes depends on those of the past, and that the bell curve is nonsense."[36] By relying on a Gaussian concept, instead of using other measures of risk, this amendment to the Basel Accord had the unforeseen consequence of actually hiding certain risks rather than highlighting them.

> " The Market Risk Amendment had the consequence of hiding certain risks rather than highlighting them. "

While ten-day VaR is useful for some purposes, such as measuring the risk of highly liquid instruments which can be exited in seconds with the touch of a keyboard, we now know it was not the right measure for highly levered AAA-rated CDOs. Clearly for these instruments another risk measure was needed.

The creators of this amendment were aware of the risks of this measurement but went ahead anyway. They did not ignore the issue; rather they sought to deal with it in a simplistic way. They thought that they could address this issue satisfactorily by using a multiplication factor. As the amendment states:

> The multiplication factor is also designed to account for potential weaknesses in the modelling process. Such weaknesses exist because:
>
> - Market price movements often display patterns (such as fat tails) that differ from the statistical simplifications used in modelling (such as the assumption of a normal distribution).
>
> - The past is not always a good approximation of the future (for example, volatilities and correlations can change abruptly).

---

[36] Benoit Mandelbrot and Richard L. Hudson, *The (Mis)behaviour of Markets* (Basic Books, 2004), p. 247.

- Value-at-risk estimates are typically based on end-of-day positions and generally do not take account of intra-day trading risk.

- Models cannot adequately capture event risk arising from exceptional market circumstances.

- Many models rely on simplifying assumptions to value the positions in the portfolio, particularly in the case of complex instruments such as options.

- When seen in the context of the other quantitative parameters, the Committee has concluded that a multiplication factor of 3 provides an appropriate and reasonable level of capital coverage to address these prudential concerns.[37]

One may well ask what the scientific basis was for using a factor of three. Reading this carefully, in retrospect, it clearly foreshadows the crisis its implementation would lay the foundation for. It helped to increase the system's confidence in its ability to predict market-based outcomes.

This amendment also stated that the minimum required period needed to determine the volatility of prices would be *one year*. In effect, regulators were looking to protect the banking system from a once-in-a-1000-year storm using a Gaussian distribution, which was known to be the wrong distribution, and by looking at one year of history and multiplying by three.

As Nasssim Taleb pithily might say, they might as well have applied astrology.

Taleb described in a damning indictment the way such thinking infects modern higher education:

> Business schools block the transmission of our practical know-how and empirical tricks and the knowledge dies with us. We learn from crisis to crisis that MPT [modern portfolio theory] has the empirical and scientific validity of astrology (without the aesthetics), yet the lessons are ignored in what is taught to 150,000 business school students worldwide.[38]

---

[37] 'Overview of the Amendment to the Capital Accord to Incorporate Market Risks', Basel Committee on Banking Supervision, January, 1996, www.bis.org/publ/bcbs23.pdf

[38] 'The pseudo-science hurting markets', *Financial Times*, 03/10/2007.

As we will see later, the leveraged use of the concepts of MPT applied to debt securities was one of the important building blocks of the shadow banking system, and led to the build up of systemic risk.

> **❝ The Market Risk Amendment would lay the foundation for the use of internal models for specific risks. ❞**

The Market Risk Amendment would lay the foundation for the use of internal models for specific risks. This meant that credit risks, in addition to market risks such as interest rate risks, could use this internal model-based approach. Initially, however, the reduction of required capital for specific risks was floored at 50% of the capital required under the "Standardised Approach".

We are now ready to examine the missing element in this regulatory history: Basel II. It would be Basel II's fate to reinforce this process by massively reducing the required capital for highly rated assets even further.

Basel II: leverage soars

The Basel II accord was published in June 2004 and led the way for the final phase in the construction of the shadow banking system. It allowed highly rated securities to require almost no capital, and encouraged a massive increase in leverage throughout the financial system. The features that Basel II introduced will now be examined.

Bear in mind that increasing leverage increases one's susceptibility to errors in predicted loss distributions. The more levered one is the less room there is for error.

On the other hand, increases in leverage allowed increases in return on capital, which is exactly what banks in a competitive environment for capital continuously try to achieve. An increase in risk like this meant in the short term much greater returns could be achieved, and much more lending capacity was available for consumers and corporations, fuelling strong economic growth, and creating the potential for a credit driven bubble. In the longer term it meant losses on capital due to a misjudgement of risk.

The Basel accords created a harmonised minimum capital requirement which was to be implemented by a certain date. As far as the Basel committee was concerned, once a general framework was agreed, the sooner the rules were implemented the better. By setting a target date, countries and institutions had flexibility as to when to implement some or all of the terms. For banks whose capital requirements would drop under the accord, they quickly implemented the rules advantageous to them.

Countries also did not necessarily implement the rules in their entirety, but instead would just ensure that their capital regulations were generally in line with the broad rules. Again, for banks whose required capital would drop, implementing those rules which reduced capital requirements was essential if they were going to increase return on capital.

> **❝ In the short term an increase in risk meant greater lending capacity was available, fuelling economic growth, and creating the potential for a credit-driven bubble. ❞**

The main impetus behind Basel II was to create a more risk-sensitive set of requirements. To that end, **credit rating agency** (CRA) ratings were chosen as the arbiters of risk. It was to be the entry of the rating agencies as players in this regulatory regime which would change the dynamics significantly, as we will see.

It should be noted that there is more than one approach for calculating capital requirements under Basel II, and the data in Table 2.2 is derived from the Internal Ratings Based (IRB) approach.

Note that now AAA-rated risk assets required extremely little capital, the goal for any banker was to get as much of their asset portfolio rated AAA as possible. This, then, was the final phase of the development of the shadow banking system.

Table 2.2: Basel II Capital Accord: RBA risk weights when the external assessment represents a long-term credit rating and/or an inferred rating derived from a long-term assessment

External rating (illustrative)	Risk weights for senior positions and eligible senior IAA exposures	Base risk weights	Risk weights for tranches backed by non-granular pools
AAA	7%	12%	20%
AA	8%	15%	25%
A+	10%	18%	35%
A	12%	20%	35%
A-	20%	35%	35%
BBB+	35%	50%	50%
BBB	60%	75%	75%
BBB-	100%	100%	100%
BB+	250%	250%	250%
BB	425%	425%	425%
BB-	650%	650%	650%
Below BB- and unrated	Deduction	Deduction	Deduction

Modern portfolio theory (MPT)

At this stage it may be helpful if we illustrate how this worked by explaining something about **modern portfolio theory (MPT)** and correlation.

Modern portfolio theory was developed by Harry Markowitz in a paper named 'Portfolio Selection' in the *Journal of Finance* in 1952. One of the main ideas behind the theory is that asset returns are not perfectly correlated. If applied to credit space, that means that if one asset defaults, it does not mean that other assets will necessarily default.

Why is this so important?

Rating agencies relied to a large extent on predicted loss distributions and probability of default to determine the ratings of structured credit securities. In order to calculate the expected loss of a **tranche** of a structured security, one must first know the probability of default and the loss, given default, for each asset in a portfolio.

Next, one must assume a correlation or relationship between defaults for each asset. By assuming lower correlation between assets, one reduces the tails of the loss distribution and the calculated risk becomes more concentrated around the expected loss. This ability to combine diversified uncorrelated assets into portfolios – concentrating the losses into less variant

> **" The combining of diversified uncorrelated assets into portfolios was key to the development of the shadow banking system. "**

predicted loss distributions, creating the possibility of increasingly bigger proportions of AAA securities – was key to the development of the shadow banking system.

For example, assume that we have two assets which are uncorrelated and which both have a one-in-ten default probability within any one-year period and an assumed total loss (100%) given default. If one asset defaults over a given period, it is reasonably likely that the other will not. Mathematically, if their events of default have no or zero correlation, the chance of both assets defaulting within one year is 1-in-100. On the other hand, the chance of one of the two assets defaulting is 18%, or nearly two times the probability of either single asset defaulting.

Therefore, by pooling these two uncorrelated assets, we increase the probability of at least one default in any given year, but decrease the probability of a complete loss of the portfolio.

This is significant because if we are right about the correlation and we are able to sell the first loss to a hedge fund or other investor, we will be left with an extremely safe, highly rated second-loss asset which is only expected to default once in 100 chances (this could be considered as once in 100 years). If the correlation assumptions are right, and the second loss piece is owned by a bank, we can expect that bank to only have a loss once per century on this type of security.

On the other hand if we are wrong about the correlation, and instead the two assets are perfectly correlated, that bank would experience a loss every ten years even on this second-loss asset. Remember, we created these from two assets which each alone are expected to default once every ten years.

It is prudent to recognise that, although we may have high confidence in our correlation predictions, these are still predictions of unknown future events. If we end up being wrong, we have built a house of cards. One of the key lessons learned through all the recent crises is that under systemic risk events, all risky assets become highly correlated. Correlation is dynamic. This shows that we need a measure of risk which can indicate our sensitivity to errors in our assumptions, such as correlation.

By pooling together assets which we assume a priori to have credit events which exhibit low correlation and then **tranching** the various cash flows from these pools, we can create a pool of securities with lower variance of losses, tranches of higher average ratings and lower minimum required capital. The most widely perceived 'free lunch' on Wall Street, diversification, became massively levered via CDOs and CDOs squared, as we will show (see p. 83).

> " One of the key lessons learned through all the recent crises is that under systemic risk events, all risky assets become highly correlated. "

In this way the final building block in the shadow banking system was put in place, and the massive leverage this facilitated created an extremely fragile banking system. If the correlation assumptions made by the rating agencies, or if the underlying loss distribution of any major component was wrong, the system would be susceptible not only to damage but to collapse.

In fact, the idea of increasing leverage across an economic system increasing the probability of higher correlation among asset prices, and increasing the correlation between asset defaults, gets to the heart of what has become known as a 'Minsky moment'. Minsky, as we shall show later, was an economist who predicted massive increases in systemic risks due to increases in leverage.

What was needed was a measure of sensitivity to errors in these predicted loss distributions.

3

Rating Agencies And The Shadow Banking System

Chapter summary

In this chapter we will go over the history of the credit-rating agencies, the role they play, the way they rate structured credit products, and how the shadow banking industry was built around them. We will also give descriptions of the new structured products the rating agencies supported. In the process we will avoid the rather simplistic condemnation of the rating agencies that has become prevalent in so many books about the crisis, and which in our view prevents a rational analysis of the root causes of the problem.

- Rating agencies play a crucial role in the fixed income markets as the accepted determiners of risk for investors, regulators and issuers. Under Basel II, regulators relinquished a substantial portion of their prudential regulation to the rating agencies.

- Financial engineers optimised capital structures according to ratings and capital regulations and developed the shadow banking system, maximising usage of money market funds as a funding source, and massively increasing leverage.

- The roles of conduits, asset-backed commercial paper (ABCP), SIVs, CDOs and monoline insurance companies in the shadow banking system are described.

Rating agencies and the use of their ratings

Credit-rating agencies (CRAs) or Nationally Recognised Statistical Ratings Organisations (NRSROs) are the mortar of the global financial infrastructure. They are used by issuers to sell bonds, by investors to judge the safety of those bonds and by regulators to protect investors. NRSROs hold the house of the financial markets together and, if their formulas crumble due to a quake, the global financial brick house becomes a house of cards – as we have seen.

So important and ubiquitous are the rating agencies that they are a de-facto regulator of the global financial industry. The entire shadow banking system is the result of confidence in the agencies and their models, and is built around their view of risk. Regulators depend on them, as do investors all around the globe.

According to Moody's website:

> John Moody & Company published Moody's Manual of Industrial and Miscellaneous Securities in 1900, the company's founding year. The manual provided information and statistics on stocks and bonds of financial institutions, government agencies, manufacturing, mining, utilities, and food companies. Within two months the publication had sold out. By 1903, circulation had exploded, and Moody's Manual was known from coast to coast [in the US].[39]

Today Moody's boasts ratings coverage of over 170,000 different securities. Moody's ratings and analyses cover more than 100 sovereign nations, 12,000 corporate issuers, 29,000 public finance issuers and 96,000 structured finance obligations. Moody's provides research to more than 9600 customer accounts at some 2400 financial institutions worldwide.[40]

Standard & Poor's is very similar in size and scope. According to their website:

> In 1860, Henry Varnum Poor published his *History of Railroads and Canals of the United States*. A founder of the financial information industry, Mr. Poor was a proponent of "the investor's right to know." In 1941, Standard Statistics merged with Poor's Publishing Company creating Standard & Poor's. Today, more than 140 years later, Standard & Poor's is the pre-eminent global provider of financial market intelligence and is still delivering on that original mission.

The total amount of outstanding debt rated by S&P globally is approximately $32 trillion, or more than two years of US GDP. "In 2007 alone, Standard & Poor's Ratings Services published more than 510,000 ratings, including 208,000 new and 302,000 revised ratings."[41]

These and other major NRSROs rate nearly every type of debt asset class in every major debt market globally. They are the number one resource for judging the safety of securities used by every participant and regulator of fixed-income markets.

The fixed-income market is enormous. It encompasses numerous different asset classes. It is made up of government bonds, municipal bonds, corporate bonds, mortgage-backed securities, credit card ABS, auto ABS, commercial mortgage-

---

[39] www.moodys.com/moodys/cust/AboutMoodys/AboutMoodys.aspx?topic=history

[40] www.moodys.com/moodys/cust/AboutMoodys/AboutMoodys.aspx?topic=intro

[41] www.standardandpoors.com

backed securities and nearly every type of debt instrument you can think of. It is used by thousands of different issuers in hundreds of countries. The scope and complexity of the fixed-income market means there is no way any individual participant can be an expert in even a small portion of the overall market. The fixed-income market provides funds for a huge number of individuals and institutions, either directly or indirectly.

All investors know it is imprudent to put all their eggs in a single basket and that, therefore, in some sense diversification in fixed income investing is the safest and soundest strategy. They also know they need exposure to the widest possible array of fixed income products in order to achieve modern portfolio theory's *efficient portfolio*, or to maximise return for a given level of risk. This is especially true in normal markets but as we noted earlier the value of this effect drops dramatically during stressed market events when risk assets become highly correlated.

> **"** The idea of uncorrelated events of default reducing variance in returns became the heart of the models used to rate the products of the shadow banking system. **"**

Modern portfolio theory suggests if we add the returns of two uncorrelated assets we own we might reduce the variance of returns in our portfolio and therefore reduce risk. This idea of uncorrelated asset returns, or uncorrelated events of default reducing variance in returns, became the heart of the correlation-based models which were used to rate the new products of the shadow banking system and facilitated a massive increase in leverage.

Investors

Of all of the players in the market, individual investors are the least equipped to analyse the wide array of securities which are available. Nonetheless, they can buy individual securities or mutual funds to help achieve their investment goals. Since all investors need to know the riskiness of a wide range of securities, they share an economic need for a trusted resource to determine the riskiness of the world's available financial instruments. This need creates a massive economy of scale for such a service provider. The rating agencies fulfil it.

If investors buy individual securities, the first thing they typically look at as a judgment of safety is the credit rating. If they invest in a mutual fund they will want to know its risk profile, which is usually described by industry categories, asset categories and rating categories. Managers are normally limited by the minimum credit rating a bond must have before they can purchase it, implying a cushion of safety for investors. Retail funds, such as money market funds, which are regulated by the Securities and Exchange Commission (SEC) in the United States, must meet certain minimum NRSRO ratings criteria. For instance, if the debt security is of short maturity and it falls in the top two rating categories offered by an agency, money market funds or 2a-7 funds can likely buy the security.[42] If the security is lower rated, they are not allowed to buy it.

> **" All investors share a need for a trusted resource to determine the riskiness of the world's available financial instruments. "**

Regulators

As credit ratings are the ubiquitous measure of safety used and trusted by investors, they are also the method of choice for determining safety by regulators. A study by the Basel committee in 2000 found that insurance, bank and securities regulators around the globe use ratings made by the rating agencies. As we also know, Basel II put agency ratings at the centre of required bank capital regulations. In a sense, the regulators in this way delegated an important part of prudential regulation to the rating agencies.

In addition to regulating money market fund investments with ratings criteria, in 1975 the SEC began using ratings to determine minimum required capital for trading assets. The United States Federal Reserve Bank uses ratings to determine in part what securities are eligible to be borrowed against and what the appropriate 'haircut', or excess collateral, must be for borrowing at the Federal Reserve discount window. The discount window is a facility open to deposit-taking banks through which they may borrow from the Federal Reserve at a pre-determined rate on pledged securities, as an emergency liquidity facility. It is also an avenue for the Federal Reserve to execute its important responsibilities as a lender of last resort.

As can be clearly seen, the rating agencies are a highly trusted resource heavily used by regulators.

---

[42] 2a-7 funds refers to money market funds which were originally regulated by the SEC under the Investment Company Act of 1940, under rule 2a-7.

Issuers

No issuer would think of issuing securities without having the seal of approval, if you will, of the rating agencies.

Due to their incredible importance, every issuer of securities lives in need of rating agencies' approval and in fear of their wrath. No issuer would ever dare to get on the wrong side of them because there is a real economic impact to this: if an issuer's rating drops below single-A long term, or A1 or A2 short term, money funds will stop lending to them, narrowing their liquidity base significantly.

In addition, under Basel II the required capital a bank must hold against an asset is often based on the rating of the asset. Therefore, a lower rating for an issue means not only that fewer investors will be interested or able to buy the asset, but also investors who still want to buy that asset may need to attribute more capital to it, which means that these investors will need a higher rate or spread in order to achieve the same return on capital. Rating agencies are key determiners of which types of investors will be able to buy the debt of a particular issuer, and what return those investors may require to buy that debt.

Every issuer knows they must have a rating and they want the highest possible rating from the agencies on any securities they issue. The higher the rating the lower the asset spread needed to interest investors. Using the new tools of structured credit products, issuers can now engineer securities with a target rating in mind, knowing what types of investors will be willing to buy securities of a particular rating and what rate of return those investors will require based on that rating.

Arbitrage and optimisation: increasing sensitivity to error

This collective acceptance of ratings by investors, securities regulators and insurance and banking regulators created a massive opportunity for financial engineers to reverse engineer securities – creating customised securities which optimally meet ratings criteria, securities regulations and investors' return hurdles.

One of the primary tools of the financial engineer is the creation of asset-backed securities. In a typical asset-backed securitisation, a group of assets are sold into a shell company or **special purpose vehicle** (SPV). These assets are themselves typically loans or bonds which are due to pay interest and principal over time. In order to fund the purchase of these assets, the SPV issues notes, usually consisting of several different classes. The different types of notes issued are called tranches; each tranche will receive a well-defined portion of the SPV's cash flows. The way the cash is distributed is typically called the waterfall. A senior tranche is senior (or first) in the cash flow waterfall, meaning it has the first claim to the asset.

If the cash flow is less than expected then senior tranches will typically get what cash is flowing, and more junior tranches get reduced cash flows or, in some cases, no cash. Equity tranches are the last in the cash flow waterfall, only getting paid if all other tranches have been paid as required. Mezzanine tranches are sandwiched between the senior tranche and the equity tranche. All of the tranches are typically referred to as asset-backed securities.

Typical ABSs are backed by auto loans, credit card receivables, residential mortgages and commercial mortgages. With the exception of commercial mortgage-backed securities (CMBS) these are granular and rather homogeneous pools of loans to private individuals. While most forms of securitisation are of phenomenal value, matching the needs of consumer borrowers with the interests of investors, some newer forms inadvertently created excessive risk.

Using the technology of securitisation, financial engineers were able to create highly tuned and, we now know, dangerous investment structures. As securities with the same ratings might have different spreads, or as pools of securities with relatively high spreads might be tranched within an SPV whereby most of the liabilities achieve a very high rating, opportunities for arbitrage occur. Differences in pricing approaches and capital requirements may allow one to buy a set of securities at a low price and sell it at a higher price in some re-packaged format. This is the definition of arbitrage. Optimisation by financial engineers minimises the cost of funding for a set of assets and

" Most forms of securitisation are valuable, matching the needs of consumer borrowers with the interests of investors, but newer forms inadvertently created excessive risk. "

creates profit opportunities for the financial engineers. Without a measure of risk which elucidates the sensitivity of these optimisations, flawed high-risk securities can result.

These arbitrage opportunities arise in part due to financial engineers' turbo-charged use of Markowitz's MPT, which we know to be delicate. Markowitz pointed out that highly diversified portfolios of assets are superior to concentrated portfolios as returns on diversified portfolios are less variant. Having a reduced loss variance on portfolios of debt meant that one could take a portfolio of high spread BBB-rated assets which are uncorrelated, slice up the returns on this portfolio into first, second and further loss pieces and then have the upper or protected slices of such a portfolio with very little or no projected losses rated AAA.

In many cases AAA-rated securities could make up the bulk of these new liabilities. By transforming a portfolio of BBB-rated assets into mostly AAA-rated securities, a financial engineer might be able to sell all of the liabilities of this new structure at a far lower spread than the BBB-rated securities paid. The financial engineer could then keep that difference for themselves; an arbitrage.

A major error, as pointed out earlier, appears to be that correlation between assets was assumed to be stable. Optimising results on this delicate concept helped to increase systemic risk.

This arbitrage and optimisation phenomenon led to the growth of the shadow banking system, essentially regulated by the free enterprise, profit-driven, rating agencies.

While rating agencies acted as the mortar of this new system, financial engineers were the architects and they worked closely with securities lawyers to execute the plan. Acting side by side, all parties worked together, carefully placing the bricks of this new financial house one on top of the other. And who had the cash to pay for the bricks? The architects designed these houses to be funded by money market funds, or the everyday cash accounts of individuals.

The shadow banking system

Not being aware of the error in using historical correlation, financial engineers looked at the demands of investors and designed products to meet those demands. The largest, cheapest and most available pool of cash liquidity in the world comes from individuals' demand accounts and, similarly, corporations' and governments' working capital accounts. Collectively, these funds invest in what is known as the money markets; highly liquid and typically highly rated low-price volatility instruments.

As noted earlier, money market funds in the US are regulated under the Investment Company Act of 1940, which regulates all mutual funds. Money market funds specifically fall under Rule 2A-7 of that act, which stipulates that the investments in such funds must be low-risk and highly rated. Money market funds must be able to redeem shares within seven days from investor demand unless there are extreme and unusual circumstances.

In practice, most money market funds allow withdrawals daily or as needed from any ATM machine. Money market funds typically pay a short-term money market interest rate, in the form of dividends paid on shares. Money market funds strive never to fall below a par market value – or in industry parlance try not to 'break the buck' – though as we shall see this is precisely what happened (see chapter six).

The two main features of money market funds, then, are safety and liquidity. Safety is regulated by Rule 2A-7 by ensuring that all investments "fall within the two top credit-rating categories of an NRSRO". Liquidity is regulated mainly by ensuring very short maturity instruments. Of course as money market funds compete with each other for the same pools of liquidity, having a comparatively higher yield would attract more investors and a larger asset base to manage, which would mean more fees for the manager. Offering investors a higher yield is therefore a good thing.

As can be seen from the Figure 3.1 and and Table 3.1, money market funds grew both incredibly quickly and to an enormous size between 1990 and 2008. By 2008 they represented nearly US$4 trillion in investor assets. Financial engineers were quick to ride this wave and opportunistically designed products to meet the growing needs of these investors, while also filling the needs of issuers, and all the time taking out a spread or fee for themselves, as they optimised products built for these funds.

Financial engineers created a shadow banking system which fell outside of a lot of banking regulation. Mortgage and loan originators offered to lend money to borrowers on a basis which they knew could be sold to investment banks for repackaging. Originators knew they would not be taking the actual credit risks of the borrowers, but were instead just receiving fees for handing money out. Banks who were originating loans for their own books found they could fund them more cheaply and attribute less regulatory capital to them if they funded them in conduits which issued CP.

Table 3.1: How large are money market funds in the US?

Year	Money market ($bn)	Growth YOY (%)
1990	498.3	
1991	542.5	8.87
1992	546.2	0.68
1993	565.3	3.50
1994	611.0	8.08
1995	753.0	23.24
1996	901.8	19.76
1997	1058.9	17.42
1998	1351.7	27.65
1999	1613.1	19.34
2000	1845.2	14.39
2001	2285.3	23.85
2002	2272.0	-0.58
2003	2051.0	-9.73
2004	1913.2	-6.72
2005	2040.5	6.65
2006	2354.8	15.40
2007	3085.8	31.04
2008	3832.3	24.19

Source: SIFMA (Securities Industry and Financial Markets Association)

Figure 3.1: Money market growth

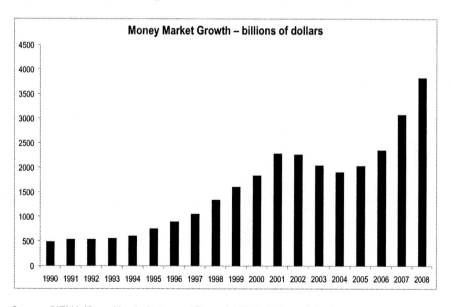

Source: SIFMA (Securities Industry and Financial Markets Association)

Investment banks and debt aggregators warehoused mortgages and levered loans while they accumulated sufficient size and diversity to securitise them and sell them as asset-backed securities, receiving fees for having built and sold the securities. AAA-rated securities were bought by SIVs which were funded in a large part by money market funds. Single A and higher-rated securities that went unsold for whatever reason might be insured by a monoline or other insurer in order to improve their rating so that they could be more easily sold to an end investor, or placed in a CP conduit.

Similarly, single A to BB-rated securities which still went unsold might be repackaged into **high grade** or mezzanine CDOs. The AAA-rated CDO paper likewise might be bought by conduits or SIVs and funded by money market funds. Lesser-rated CDO tranches might be bought by banks or other CDOs. CDO equity might be sold to hedge funds as highly levered investments, or might be kept by investment banks if they were valued at less than the fees they received to create the CDOs.

In each step of the process banks earned fees, and converted the debt into highly rated securities which could be bought on a highly levered basis by banks or insurance companies and/or funded by money market funds.

As we will see later, there was an inherent increase in leverage, in addition to a tapping of the very deep base of money market funds for funding these securities. This process of converting lowly-rated illiquid debt into highly rated liquid debt meant that there was an almost unquenchable demand for debt to be securitised. As demand outstripped supply, credit spreads fell to historically low levels, and the quality of the supply of new loans dropped as originators tried to find more creative ways of keeping up with the demand for loans to be securitised. This created massive support for the bubble that developed in the US housing and leveraged loan markets.

ABCP: short term, low risk and high liquidity

According to *The Journal of Structured and Project Finance*, asset-backed commercial paper (ABCP) conduits were first established in 1985. As with many products in the securitisation and shadow banking world, these vehicles are flexible and help to finance much of the debt that is used today. They also help to finance residential mortgages, auto loans, credit cards, student loans, equipment leases, aviation equipment, films, corporate loans and many other activities.

ABCP goes a long way to filling the needs of investors who require short-term, low risk and highly liquid investments.

Figure 3.2: Growth of US ABCP issuance volumes

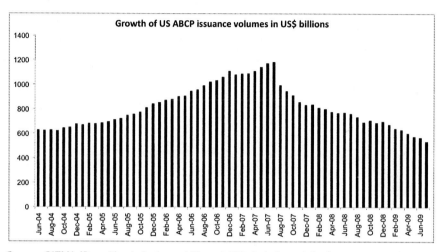

Source: SIFMA (Securities Industry and Financial Markets Association)

Table 3.2: Growth of US ABCP issuance volumes in US$ billions

	2004	2005	2006	2007	2008	2009
Jan	-	674.1	859.6	1,084.9	840.9	677.2
Feb	-	686.2	877.4	1,090.4	814.8	646.1
Mar	-	683.7	884.3	1,094.0	806.7	635.2
Apr	-	690.8	906.0	1,115.8	783.4	605.5
May	-	700.5	912.2	1,147.4	773.6	579.7
Jun	632.4	715.3	950.9	1,175.7	775.4	572.6
Jul	627.4	728.3	962.4	1,186.5	767.2	539.0
Aug	630.5	753.3	997.1	999.4	738.9	-
Sep	624.2	764.4	1,024.3	950.5	697.3	-
Oct	647.7	780.1	1,039.2	917.2	712.7	-
Nov	654.1	816.5	1,064.8	860.1	693.7	-
Dec	679.6	848.0	1,112.8	838.7	704.5	-

Source: Federal Reserve System

As can be clearly seen from Figure 3.2 and Table 3.2, ABCP issuance exploded from 2004 until the peak in the summer of 2007, growing as much as 31%

year-on-year and reaching its crest at nearly US$1.2 trillion. ABCP issuance grew in step with the rising demand of investors; in particular, money market funds. Issuance nearly doubled between the summer of 2004 and the summer of 2007, and then, just as soon as investor confidence in these vehicles fell, ABCP issuance collapsed.

How do ABCP conduits work?

Figure 3.3: A SIV capital structure

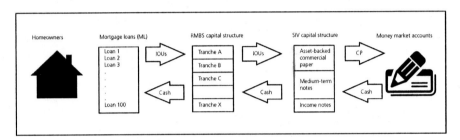

Let's say you're a bank or hedge fund and you think a certain set of bonds or loans offer a relatively high spread and yet are very safe or creditworthy. When you look at the yields on them they look relatively high, especially against money market rates. One way for you to take advantage of this opportunity is to buy the bonds or loans and put them into a **special purpose entity** (SPE), fund that vehicle by issuing very low spread commercial paper and sell that CP to money market funds.

An investor of financial assets, i.e. a bank or hedge fund, will set up an SPE which buys appealing assets. This SPE will be made safe or credit worthy for CP investors in any number of different ways. One way is over-collateralisation, whereby the SPE will have assets worth more than the amount of CP issued to investors. Another is to ensure the assets the SPE owns yield far more than what the SPE pays to CP investors for funding. The excess spread generated from this difference might be trapped within the vehicle as a cash flow cushion to protect CP investors. The SPE might have reserve accounts with extra cash. The SPE could get a small amount of first loss protection from the originator, say 1% or 2%. Finally, the SPE could have some of the assets it invests in guaranteed by an insurance company.

In addition to looking at the SPE's credit enhancements in order to evaluate the safety or creditworthiness of the conduit, rating agencies also ensure there is always enough cash to pay off the current CP holders. There is typically a large mismatch between the long maturities of the assets purchased and the very short-dated (typically 30 days) CP liabilities which are issued. This maturity mismatch means that the programme is subject to the risk that the issuer may not be able to roll or sell their CP to money market investors, which would mean they would not be able to pay off their current CP investors in time.

Of course the reason a conduit sponsor would promote this is to make money. The longer the maturity of a bond, the higher the spread it pays to investors. In reverse, the shorter the funding or CP issued, typically the lower the required spread. Therefore the bigger the maturity mismatch, the more excess spread and the more money the sponsor makes.

In order to address this maturity mismatch or liquidity risk, CP conduits usually require liquidity support from highly-rated banks, guaranteeing the CP will be paid off on time by either providing liquidity as needed against individual assets or against the entire programme. As we saw earlier, under Basel I as long as the maturity of the liquidity line was shorter than one year no regulatory capital was required whatsoever. This absence of any measured capital requirement made this an extremely interesting prospect as returns on capital would therefore be great. It meant that banks could increase leverage without that leverage being measured, monitored or regulated.

> " ABCP vehicles have played a major role in today's financial markets, funding consumer and corporate credit needs and filling money market and institutional investor needs. "

As conduits typically have very thin first-loss protection, their creditworthiness (outside of liquidity considerations) is driven by the high quality of the assets they buy. The assets of credit arbitrage conduits are very often dominated by AAA-rated paper. The asset classes purchased include CDOs, mortgages, auto loans and leases, credit card debt, equipment leases, student loans, etc.

Some arbitrage conduits are dominated by one asset class or another and, depending upon the class, the underlying risk profile can be substantially different. Like SIVs (see next section) they rely upon eligibility criteria, and selling of assets if assets fail to meet those criteria, in order to maintain creditworthiness.

There is no doubt from the above that these ABCP vehicles have played a major role in today's financial markets, funding consumer and corporate credit needs and filling money market and institutional investor needs.

Structured investment vehicles (SIVs)

Another major issuer of ABCP during this time was structured investment vehicles or SIVs. SIVs were invented by Stephen Partridge-Hicks in 1990 while he was at Citibank as another way of taking advantage of the deep and cheap liquidity available in money market funds and in demand accounts of institutional investors. More than a decade after their invention, some SIVs began purchasing new and riskier securities, which would put an end to investor confidence in these structures. By July 2007, SIVs funded approximately $370 billion in assets.[43]

Like conduits, SIVs were set up by banks or hedge funds as a way to get cheap financing or leverage from money market funds to fund a pool of assets they felt were also cheap and to earn a levered return. There are, however, a number of differences with conduits.

SIVs would generate most of their credit protection by selling income notes which would provide considerable first loss protection, of say 8% or so. SIVs would issue short-term CP for cheap financing just like conduits, but SIVs would also issue longer-term notes, or medium-term notes, with maturities longer than a year. Thus they reduced their need to roll-over shorter-term commercial paper.

This longer-term funding profile used by SIVs meant that they did not need to have a liquidity provider for all of the assets in the programme to protect the CP investors, but could instead have just a small percentage of their total issuance covered by emergency bank liquidity lines.

Another critical difference and safety measure in SIVs was their need to mark to market their assets and their obligation to keep the market value of those assets above the total par value of the CP and medium-term notes issued. This meant that if some of the assets did not perform well, those assets would be closely monitored. If the value of the assets fell far enough to risk their value slipping below the value of the issued CP and medium-term notes, the manager may have been required to sell assets, forcing the income notes to take the loss and protecting the CP and medium-term note holders.

In the summer of 2007 investors lost faith in ABCP and there was a massive run on SIVs and ABCP conduits. Imagine what happened during that summer

---

[43] Birgit Sprecht, Sophia Kauntze and Jonathon M Neve, 'Fixed Income Quantitative Research European Securitised Products Strategy', Citigroup Global Markets Ltd, 3 August 2007.

as ABCP issuance fell from US$1186 billion to US$860 billion in just four months. Issuers needed to find $326 billion in funding from alternative sources! This was a run which was completely unexpected and had the potential to bring down the financial system.

The reason for this is that money needed to be raised very quickly and the amount was more than any set of banks would normally have readily available. In addition, these vehicles fell outside the normal jurisdiction of the Federal Reserve's lender of last resort mandate. Therefore the system risked, and to some extent experienced, a de-leveraging: conduits and banks needed to sell assets to raise funds, which then lowered the price of assets, which caused more fear in investors and caused investors to buy less ABCP, forcing more liquidations. A vicious self-feeding cycle of selling, followed by lower asset prices, followed by more selling, ensued.

What did the SIVs buy?

Much like arbitrage conduits, SIVs mostly bought very highly-rated paper in order to ensure that the credit risk, or expected losses from credit risk, would be extremely low. This concentration on highly-rated assets also ensured that the SIVs could issue highly-rated commercial paper which would be bought by money market funds. The assets they bought were dominated by AAA and AA-rated paper, with very small amounts of A and lower-rated paper.

The asset classes they purchased included debt of financials (especially subordinated debt), residential-mortgage-backed securities, CDOs, commercial mortgage-backed securities, credit-card-backed securities, student-loan-backed securities and other asset-backed securities. In general they bought highly-rated financials and asset-backed securities which had very low expected credit losses as per ratings agency models.

Many years after the founding of the SIV market a number of new SIVs were built. As spreads fell dramatically, in some cases more highly levered but highly rated assets were purchased by SIVs in order to ensure positive carry. Seemingly it was the later entrants with the more highly levered assets who had the first and most immediate problems when liquidity vanished.

Who bought the income notes and why?

Income notes, or the part of the capital structure which would absorb the first losses of the asset portfolio once excess spread was exhausted, were often bought by financial institutions. These income notes could generate a very high return, often in the high single digits to low double digits.

Even though these notes were levered as many as 12 times (even before considering the leverage embedded in the underlying assets), they retained a high rating – generally BBB. This is mainly due to the fact that they invested in very highly-rated assets.

In some cases banks may have been able to count just 8% capital against these notes and in many cases they were probably required to take a full capital deduction or to put 100% capital against them.

If they only held 8% capital against them, in a sense they would allow a bank to square its leverage versus old capital rules. Under old capital rules a bank could lever itself 12 times. If a bank was required to hold only 8% capital against the notes, then the normal 12 times leverage could be multiplied by the 12 times leverage of the notes for 144 times leverage.

Another factor to keep in mind is that many of the assets purchased by SIVs were themselves already levered – maybe to the order of 40 times. Looking at this additional layer we notice that the leverage is further compounded.

This means that a financial institution may have be able to achieve leverage of 12 times 40, or 480 times, if a full capital deduction was required on the income notes. If they only held 8% capital against the income notes, then they could have been levered thousands of times. This layering of leverage massively increased the underlying risk beyond that implied by the nominal leverage.

Of further concern is the fact that much of the financials debt that SIVs purchased was subordinated debt.

A SIV may have owned as much as 40% financials (bank and insurance company) subordinated debt. And all the income notes issued by an SIV could potentially have been purchased by the same or related financials whose subordinated debt had been purchased by the SIV.

> **Example**
>
> If we assume a total SIV with a size of US$10 billion then the SIV might own US$4 billion of financials sub-debt. In return those same financials could buy all the first loss income notes for 8% of the capital structure, or US$0.8 billion. That US$0.8 billion of investments made by financial institutions might only require 8%, or US$0.064 billion, of capital. So the financial system could generate US$4 billion of new subordinated debt, a form of capital, while taking the first loss piece of the entire structure.
>
> This is, of course, a financial house of mirrors. No new capital ever entered the system yet new capital could be reported on banks' books. Imagine what would happen, then, to the commercial-paper holders (money market funds) if there was a loss of 8%.
>
> All of the financial institutions would wipe out a portion of their capital, which would possibly mean that some may not be able to pay on their subordinated debt, which would mean losses to the CP holders.

The fact that financial institutions were providing first-loss protection on a portfolio of financial institutions' subordinated debt had the potential to create a house of cards. Normally, financial institutions would hold only very small amounts of other financial institutions' subordinated debt as this would generally create a capital deduction for the purchasing financial institution in order to avoid systemic risk.

Income notes from SIVs, however, seem to have avoided this. Seemingly it would be possible for ABC bank to own the income notes or the first loss piece of a SIV which was heavily invested in XYZ bank subordinated debt, and likewise, XYZ bank could own the income notes of an SIV which was heavily invested in the subordinated debt of ABC bank. This is apropos of an equity cross shareholding which we will show is an extremely fragile structure. By their very nature SIVs had the potential to add to systemic risk.

> " Normally, financial institutions would hold only very small amounts of other financial institutions' subordinated debt. SIVs seem not to have followed this practice. "

The risk in equity cross-holding

If two financial institutions buy equity in each other and if this is then reported as capital in each, excessive leverage can be achieved. We saw earlier how the cross shareholdings between Japanese financial institutions, which were an important characteristic of the 1980s boom – and bust – in Japanese share and land prices, created a very fragile situation. Subordinated debt cross-holdings like this might also have been possible in SIVs.

Imagine ABC bank buys US$100 million of equity in XYZ bank and XYZ bank buys US$100 million of equity in ABC bank. Note: there is no real cash to start with and no real capital is generated as each simply issue paper to the other.

Assume then that XYZ bank incurs credit losses of US$100 million. ABC might lose its US$100 million equity investment in XYZ. These losses could of course be absorbed by XYZ bank's equity holding of ABC bank, incurring further loss of US$100 million in XYZ bank. So, a US$100 million loss in XYZ bank can double.

Any cross shareholding has the potential to create an overstatement of economic capital. In the new language of risk we introduce later in the book, this type of cross shareholding creates an infinite loop of multiplications in its calculation of risk, making evident the risk this type of arrangement creates.

This is the reason why any holding of subordinated debt by a bank, in another bank, generally receives a full capital deduction for the purchasing bank in most jurisdictions. None the less this basic rule seems to have been circumvented when measuring the capital required to purchase SIV income notes.

Let us now look at CDOs, the assets they would buy and their capital structure, and how they might issue CPs.

Collateralised debt obligations (CDOs)

Collateralised debt obligations (CDOs), like any other asset-backed security, had the essential elements of an asset pool which was purchased and placed within a special purpose vehicle (SPV).[44] The SPV would be considered

---

[44] An SPV, sometimes referred to as a special purpose entity or SPE, is typically a limited purpose company set up with a very narrow set of objectives, such as to hold financial assets and issue notes which are paid out of the proceeds of the assets.

bankruptcy remote and all the assets would be considered to have been placed in the SPV as a 'true sale'. In order to fund the purchase of those securities, the CDO would need to have a capital structure with a clearly defined hierarchy of seniority in events of loss. That capital structure would generally have an equity or first-loss piece, and then mezzanine tranches which would absorb losses after the equity was exhausted.

Figure 3.4: How CDOs work

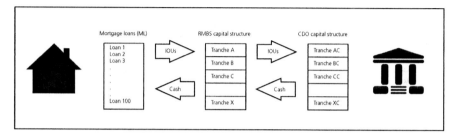

If, for some reason, the mezzanine layers or tranches of the capital structure were wiped out, then the senior layers or tranches would incur losses. In reverse, of course, senior tranches had equity and mezzanine layers below them as protection from losses in that asset's portfolio.

As the equity portion of the capital structure incurs the most risk, it would be expected to have the highest yield initially in order to compensate for the fact that it was taking the highest risk. Likewise, the mezzanine tranches would be expected to have a yield lower than the equity but higher than the senior tranches, as the risk was lower than equity but higher than the senior tranches.

In terms of nomenclature, the equity tranche or layer would begin to absorb the first losses, so it was considered to attach to losses at 0% (or to have an **attachment point** of 0%). If the equity represented 3% of the capital structure it would then detach from losses at 3% (or have a **detachment point** of 3%), or it would be wiped out after 3% of the asset portfolio was lost. Similarly, the mezzanine portion of the capital structure might attach at 3%, be 6% wide and detach at 9%. This means that it would begin to absorb losses after 3% of the capital structure had already been wiped out by losses and it would continue to absorb all the losses above that until 9% of the capital structure was wiped out.

Similarly, the senior tranche may attach at 9% and detach at 100%. That means it would not begin to absorb losses until 9% was already wiped out. Likewise, it would absorb all losses above 9% to 100%. The absorption of losses would be very clearly defined in CDO documentation, according to various tests which would turn off cash flows, interest and principal, according to very specific rules.

CDOs can have enormous flexibility as a product class and offer investors many positive attributes. The underlying assets purchased can be of many different classes: asset-backed securities, emerging market bonds, corporate bonds, financials bonds, levered loans and almost any type of debt you can imagine.

In addition, the SPV issuing the CDOs can be managed or static. If the investor thought that a manager could add value by picking securities which would be purchased or sold for a CDO, using its financial acumen to avoid any credit losses, this could be arranged and a fee would be paid to that manager to actively manage the asset pool. If the investors thought that the skill of a manager in avoiding losses will not outweigh the costs of its fees, then a deal might be static.

Similarly, the assets and liabilities of a CDO might be either funded or synthetic. If an investor wanted to put cash to work, they might buy cash securities issued by a CDO, which that CDO would then invest in securities. Those securities might represent the bulk or all of the risk in the CDO or they might only represent a small part. The CDO might, in addition to buying cash securities, sell credit default swap protection on a portfolio of securities in an unfunded format. In addition, the investor might want to sell protection on a portfolio of securities through a CDS contract in an unfunded or synthetic format.

A deal might also be a hybrid deal – meaning that some of the assets would be cash assets and some might be in synthetic or derivative form. Likewise, some of the liabilities might be in the form of cash, presumably enough to purchase the cash assets, and there may be synthetic or derivative liabilities to cover the synthetic assets.

CDOs are often categorised by the type of assets they purchase. A **collateralised loan obligation** (CLO) is a CDO which invests primarily in leveraged loans. A structured finance or ABS CDO would be one which invests primarily in asset-backed securities. A mezzanine ABS CDO would invest mainly in low investment grade (typically BBB average weighted rating) mezzanine tranches of asset-backed securities. A high-grade ABS CDO would invest in A to AA-weighted average rating asset-backed security tranches. Both mezzanine and high-grade CDOs had the ability to buy tranches of other ABS CDOs.

A collateralised synthetic obligation (CSO) would typically be purely a derivative contract referencing credits. A typical corporate CSO might reference the senior bond debt of 125 different corporations. It would then be tranched similarly to other ABS securities.

Enter the monoline insurers

Another key category of player in the shadow banking system is the monoline insurance industry. On a practical level, like many elements of the shadow banking system, monoline insurers are inherently regulated by the rating agencies. Monoline insurers such as the Municipal Bond Insurance Association (MBIA), which was founded in 1973, and the American Municipal Bond Assurance Corporation (AMBAC), which was founded in 1971, play a critical role for investors not dissimilar to the role played by rating agencies.

Monoline insurers provide enormous economies of scale within the financial markets. There are over 50,000 different issuers of municipal bonds in the United States. This means that, much like the total number of fixed-income asset classes available to investors, there is no way any small organisation can track the creditworthiness of all these issuers.

Rating agencies play a key role for investors who do not have the time or expertise to follow all these issuers by offering a rating scale which is supposed to indicate quality across all these bonds. Even though some individual investors who typically invest in municipal bonds because of their special tax-exempt status may be willing to buy bonds which are of less than the highest quality, AAA, most investors prefer only to buy AAA-rated securities.

Monoline insurance companies guarantee investment-grade municipal bonds, so that investors can rely not just on the municipal entities' willingness and ability to pay, but on the monoline insurer's willingness and ability to pay in the case of a default of the municipal issuer. As most monoline insurers were rated AAA up until the recent credit crisis, this guarantee made investors lives much easier: they could buy a wide variety of bonds issued by municipal entities in their own state, all of the highest credit quality.

Knowing that a monoline insurer has backed a municipal bond has several advantages:

- The bond is known to be of the highest credit quality.

- If a bond issuer which has been guaranteed by a monoline begins to have financial problems, the monoline has enough size all on its own to justify the legal fees and negotiations which may be needed with that municipal issuer to ensure the bond holders got the best possible deal in a difficult situation.

- Having a monoline behind an issuer means that the monoline has done its own independent analysis, which also acts as another assurance that the bond is of high quality in addition to the ratings agency ratings.

- As individual investors get the greatest tax benefit from investing in the municipal bonds issued by their states only, attaining the most tax benefit inherently means that investors are encouraged to have a geographic concentration and cannot follow the best practice of achieving high diversification. By having monolines which insure bonds across the entire country, the individual investor indirectly gets the benefit of the geographic diversity of the monolines.

However monolines, in retrospect in error, got into the business of guaranteeing structured finance securities as well. This allowed monolines to massively increase their revenues by issuing guarantees on a further set of uncorrelated assets. Guaranteeing these securities for banks meant allowing banks to eliminate much, or in some cases all, regulatory capital needed for these securities even if they continued to be funded by the banks.

> **" By guaranteeing structured finance securities, monolines allowed banks to eliminate much of the regulatory capital needed for these securities. "**

The monolines insured assets placed in conduits, assuring that they were of the highest credit rating. They insured subprime mortgages, making them safe for investors, and facilitated conduits, SIVs, and CDOs in attaining target ratings needed to issue commercial paper which could be bought by money market funds. Their AAA-rated guarantees meant that – under Basel II – a bank might only need to hold 7% times 8% or 56 basis points (bps)[45] in capital

---

[45] A basis point is equal to one-hundredth of a percent, and is regularly used to define the amount of change in a financial instrument.

for a slice of a CDO guaranteed by a monoline if it were held in a banking book. If it were held in a trading book, the amount of capital may have been much lower than that. This is due to the fact that AAA-rated assets typically had very little volatility in price.

This very low price volatility would mean a very low VaR and therefore very little required capital. In the extreme, some believed that an AAA wrap from a monoline on an AAA-rated tranche of a CDO meant that no capital was needed as the expected loss was very nearly zero.

For monolines, this new business meant revenues and an area for growth of assets they were guaranteeing. These new exposures were also thought by the monolines' inherent regulator, the rating agencies, to be less than perfectly correlated with their existing line of municipal business and therefore added a significant diversification benefit.

Not to be left out, certain insurance companies – with their AAA credit ratings – decided to join the game, guaranteeing super senior tranches of ABS CDOs and, arguably, they became the biggest player by far.

One insurance company in particular sold CDS protection on tens of billions of AAA-rated super senior tranches of mezzanine and high-grade ABS CDOs, which both they and the rating agencies thought would never experience any losses. Of course, one should never say never and the enormous leverage that the tens of billions of CDSs represented, and even more the further leverage represented by the underlying structures, eventually led to the need for a massive government bailout.

In summary, then, the shadow banking system looked something like this:

Assets were pooled into special purpose vehicles, which then issued notes that represented different layers in the capital structure of the SPV. The top slice was very often funded by money market funds as long as it was highly enough rated by the rating agencies. Money market funds represented the largest and cheapest pool of cash liquidity. If those assets were not highly enough rated, they might be wrapped by a monoline or insurer. Any SPV liabilities taken onto bank balance sheets would require capital which was implicitly determined by the rating agencies.

The rating agencies were the mortar holding together the new system – they determined what was safe for investors and especially money market funds. As we will see in the next chapter, the regulators relied on the agencies as well, to determine what capital the banks needed. In a sense, financial regulators globally relinquished their responsibilities of prudential regulation to the rating agencies. Clearly that approach has failed and a radical new approach is needed.

4

How The Current System Failed And The Need For See-Through Leverage (STL)

Chapter summary

- The drive of banks to optimise short-term return on capital (ROC) for equity investors motivated the creation of the shadow banking system.

- Basel II addressed some of the flaws of Basel I by making capital requirements more sensitive to expected losses, while increasing risk due to leverage.

- New structures of the shadow banking system in combination with Basel regulations allowed a massive drop in required capital for the same level of risk.

- The combination of ratings, regulations and financial engineering facilitated a massive increase in leverage.

- A new language of risk – see-through leverage or the family of STL risk indices – is introduced, which simply and easily makes the massive increase in risk completely transparent.

Confidence destroyed

The 2007-2009 banking crisis destroyed confidence in the global financial system. Governments across the world reacted by stepping in to stabilise banks and insurance companies to prevent runs on banks, a collapse in lending and a massive fall in economic growth similar to the Great Depression. Yet, fundamentally, the problem of a lack of confidence remains. A radical cure, which attacks the cause of the crisis, is what is needed.

> **STL helps lead to a better understanding of the risk of structured securities of all ratings.**

See-through leverage, or STL, is a groundbreaking new concept in financial thought. STL works by measuring risk in a completely new way and allows investors to differentiate between healthy AAA-rated and potentially toxic but nonetheless AAA-rated securities. In fact, STL helps lead to a better understanding of the risk of structured securities of all ratings. The STL index will be of enormous significance to the new world of finance, risk management, asset securitisation, banking regulation and investment.

Embracing STL requires a key conceptual shift in the way in which we perceive the measurement of risk. Astronomers before Copernicus and Galileo tried to predict the motion of the planets. Although these astronomers did well, they eventually found that their calculations were far off and, in general, always mistaken. They tried many ad hoc fixes to adjust their predictions, but nothing quite worked. The key conceptual paradigm shift which Copernicus, and later Galileo, embraced was to place the sun at the centre of the planets instead of the earth. This epiphany simplified everything, to such an extent that every school child now looks at those same planets as the *solar* system.

Regulatory capital for asset securitisation products, and indeed for all structured credit products, is primarily based upon ratings. Those ratings are based primarily on the amount of subordination, or first-loss protection, sitting below the investment being rated. Standard & Poor's, in particular, at one point explicitly rated all securitisation products based on the estimated probability of the first dollar of loss. Thus, every regulator and investor is focused on the amount of subordination as the centre of the finance universe.

STL moves the centre of the banking regulation universe. Instead of focusing on and measuring the amount of subordination junior to an investment, STL focuses on the amount of liabilities senior to the investment: this is the mathematical finance, regulatory and rating equivalent of placing the sun, rather than the earth, at the centre of the universe.

Let's rewind a little to the lending bubble. The bubble preceding the 2007-2009 crisis was characterised by a massive increase in lending driven, in large part, by the growth of securitisation. As mentioned earlier, American asset-backed securities outstanding in 1990 were just US$100 billion; by the end of 2000, the figure was US$900 billion; and by June 2008 this had risen to US$2498 billion, representing a 19.5% annualised growth rate for 18 years. According to Dealogic, by 2007 more than half of all the money borrowed in the US credit markets was borrowed either through asset-backed securities or by securitisation.

How could there have been such a large increase in lending via securitisation? And where did all the required capital come from? Was there a massive increase in capital seeking risk, or was something else happening?

In fact, there was no massive growth in capital available, but there was a massive increase in leverage. The regulators, together with the market participants, had effectively stopped measuring leverage.

STL pinpoints excessive leverage and is, mathematically, a measure of a product's sensitivity to assumptions or confidence in the underlying asset pool's loss distribution. When a security's STL is high, it means that the underlying leverage is high. Leverage, as we have pointed out, will magnify both gains and losses. High leverage, therefore, requires extreme confidence in one's assumptions when making an investment. In essence, STL strips away the distortions introduced by shadow banking, the inadequacies of the rating agencies and the weakness of Basel II in measuring risk in an asset.

We can calculate STL for many of the products of the shadow banking system, and can show a direct correlation between risk and STL. Without building any complex models, and while ignoring the

> **" STL pinpoints excessive leverage and is a mathematical measure of a product's sensitivity to assumptions in the underlying asset pool's loss distribution. "**

underlying asset class, STL alone is, retrospectively, able to explain nearly half of the variation in downgrades in a wide variety of ABS securities. We will show how high STL securities were inevitably downgraded many notches, and how they incurred massive losses for investors. Under Basel II such losses meant an enormous required capital increase for banks, which is now being provided by taxpayers.

Risk weighting under Basel

As we have seen, in 1988 the Basel committee of senior representatives of bank supervisory authorities and central banks from the G10 countries agreed on Basel I, which was intended to make certain minimum capital requirements for international banks uniform across national borders. It was motivated in part by the 1974 collapse of Cologne-based Bank Herstatt, which had the potential to cause a financial crisis across borders.

A key aspect of Basel I was its replacement of simple asset-based leverage measures with a concept known as risk weighted assets (RWA). As discussed earlier, however, under Basel I, each asset type would be categorised according to credit risk type and then given a risk weighting (RW). Once a RW was assigned, each bank would be required to have capital enough to cover 8% of RWA.

For a reminder of different risk weights by category of on-balance-sheet asset, see Table 2.1 on p. 35.

Maximising a bank's return on capital (ROC): growth of off-balance-sheet securitisation structures

Banks, of course, had an interest in maximising their return on capital (ROC) in order to ensure that they achieved attractive returns for their equity investors. In particular, banks achieving higher ROC would clearly be better able to compete for capital and could grow more quickly. Securitisation experts followed the mantra of innovation, and began asking how various structures might be interpreted under these new capital rules.

At the same time, the available tools of securitisation began to take off. This was facilitated by an enormous increase in computing power and the use of modelling. As computer software became more sophisticated, financial modelling moved in lockstep. Technological innovation and the speed of information dissemination all played a role.

Several types of structures were then proposed and many of these were implemented to maximise ROC under the new Basel I RWA rules. The common theme among all of them was that they allowed banks to further leverage themselves and remain within the new capital guidelines. These innovations were introduced by structurers in many banks in many countries. Securitisation exploded as a new tool. These new balance-sheet tools took various forms. One, for example, was the simple two-tranche structure of which JP Morgan's famous Bistro series was best known.

We will describe all structures in a stylised manner in order not to get too bogged down in the complex details. The main point is to appraise the overall impact on leverage.

Let's say that a bank started with a highly diversified portfolio of loans, generally corporate, which has a 100% RW. Under Basel I, the bank would have been required to set aside capital equal to 8% times 100% of the amount of the loans.

Using securitisation techniques, those same loans could be moved off-balance-sheet onto a separate special purpose vehicle (SPV) which issued paper that referenced said loans; in effect, investors were allowed to participate in the risk and returns of that portfolio. It was not a straightforward pass through of cash flows. The structure would have at least two tranches; a junior tranche and a senior tranche.

The junior tranche would typically receive a very high coupon, but in return for absorbing, say, the first 8% of losses in the entire portfolio. As the senior tranche is 'protected' from the first 8% of the losses, the mathematical models would suggest that the senior tranche would be highly unlikely ever to experience any losses. As such, the senior tranche would be very highly rated but would receive a much lower coupon. A sponsoring bank might then keep the junior tranche (8% of face of total assets) and sell the senior tranche (the other 92% of face of total assets) to outside investors. In effect, since the sponsoring bank nominally owns only the face amount of the junior tranche, it would report only 8% of the total face amount of the loans as an asset on its balance sheet.

Under Basel I rules, this structure might allow the sponsoring bank to reduce the capital requirement from 8% of total assets to a requirement of 0.64% of assets (i.e. 8% x 8%) while bearing all of the expected risk. At a minimum this would create a question for regulators, as the Basel I rules interpreted this way would allow a massive increase in risk. In response some regulators would require a full capital deduction against this, reducing the opportunity for leverage.

This, however, created another potential opportunity. Say instead that the bank was securitising a very highly rated portfolio of loans. The bank might then be able to create a structure where the senior tranche may only need 4% subordination to achieve an AAA rating from rating agencies. That AAA-rated paper might be very easy to sell at a very low spread, leaving the bank with a very high coupon equity or first loss piece.

In this case, even if a seemingly onerous full capital deduction was required, the bank would be better off. It would have retained the bulk of the risk and return and it would only need to put 4%, or half the amount, of capital normally required.

The sponsoring bank above would have done just what its equity investors wanted: it increased its leverage and therefore its return on capital. And it did so by a simple repackaging of its balance-sheet assets. These issues were certainly some of the stimuli behind the creation of Basel II, which used credit ratings as the arbiters of risk.

Basel II: using credit ratings as a measure of risk

Banking regulators became aware of the plethora of new securitisation structures which were being established under the Basel I rules. While they perceived Basel I as a success at making capital requirements more uniform across OECD borders, they also saw how they had allowed banks to take more risks, becoming more highly levered, as an unintended consequence. In order to address this concern, in 2004 the Basel Committee on Banking Supervision published a second Basel Accord: Basel II. Specifically, they wanted to reduce the regulatory capital arbitrage allowed under Basel I, or to make capital requirements more risk sensitive.

In order to make capital requirements more risk sensitive, the decision makers decided to use a graduated scale of RWs depending on the underlying risk, as measured by the asset's credit rating. As a consequence, the risk-sensitive framework depended on the robustness of the independent Nationally Recognised Statistical Rating Organisations (NSROs) as the judges of risk. One of the consequences of this was that the RWs were now driven by the ratings.

> **Basel II was designed to reduce the regulatory capital arbitrage allowed under Basel I, or to make capital requirements more risk sensitive.**

Under Basel II, an AAA-rated ABS tranche would have a RW of 7% to 20%. This meant that a most senior AAA-rated tranche may only require 7% times 8%, or 56bps, of capital, allowing far greater leverage. AA tranches would have RWs of 8% to 25%. Non-investment grade tranches would be a full capital deduction.

For securitisation vehicles, rating agencies examined the known history of defaults and recoveries for each asset type and determined a loss distribution for a pool. After the pool's loss distribution was determined, the rating agencies then attributed these losses to the tranched liabilities which made up the capital structure. If the subordination of a tranche exceeded any stressed case loss in the predicted loss distribution then, by definition, it would have to be rated AAA as they could not find any case where it would experience a loss.

Here, then, was a significant example of intellectual legerdemain. The main driver of tranche ratings was the predicted loss distribution of the asset pool or stressed case losses as estimated by the rating agencies. Standard & Poor's explicitly used the concept of the probability of the first dollar of loss of a certain tranche in order to determine a risk rating of that tranche. Fitch did as well. Moody's similarly would determine the amount of subordination needed for a specific asset pool in order to match the expected loss of a tranche of a certain thickness with a target expected loss associated with a particular rating grade.

Apparently, however, the rating agencies did not explicitly use leverage as a rating factor to rate securitisation structures.

So Basel II, while hoping to create a more risk-sensitive regulatory capital framework, in fact had the unintended consequence of significantly increasing risk by facilitating the possibility of a massive increase in leverage. Since Basel II specifies a capital requirement based upon the rating of an ABS tranche, it inherently bases capital requirements on the expected losses of a particular security derived from a history of losses of similar securities. As seen in the credit crisis, the expected loss of a security is highly vulnerable to the business cycle, and one can argue ratings would be more appropriately used to determine required reserves than capital. Capital requirements should inherently be more about how the actual loss may be significantly worse than the expected loss.

None the less, the history of losses was used to predict the future loss distribution. And as Nassim Taleb has pointed out again and again, black swans do indeed exist and we are in general not capable of predicting loss distributions. In order, therefore, to determine the risk of a large error in the predicted distribution, we need another family of risk indices – STL.

Let us explain what we mean.

In order to fund subprime mortgages and reduce the required RWA, banks would securitise them. Table 4.1 is a typical capital structure for one of these deals. (The Basel II risk weightings used in all tables in this chapter are those as per the IRB approach mentioned earlier.)

Table 4.1: A typical capital structure for a subprime mortgage securitisation deal

Scenario A: Basel I

	Risk Weighting (%)	Size (%)	Amount (US$m)	RWA (US$m)
Pool of Subprime	50	100.00	1000	**500**

Scenario B: Basel II

Tranche Rating	Risk Weighting (%)	Size (%)	Amount (US$m)	RWA (US$m)
AAA	7	23.00	230	16.1
AAA	12	56.00	560	67.2
AA+	15	7.00	70	10.5
AA	15	2.00	20	3
AA-	15	2.00	20	3
A+	18	1.80	18	3.24
A	20	1.50	15	3
A-	35	1.50	15	5.25
BBB+	50	1.50	15	7.5
BBB	75	1.60	16	12
BBB-	100	0.40	4	4
BB+	250	0.40	4	10
Sub-total Non equity		98.70	987	144.79
Equity	1250	1.30	13	162.5
Total		100.00	1000	**307.29**
Ex equity				144.79
Ex equity & AAA				61.49

As can be seen from Table 4.1, the simple act of securitisation could drop the RWA from US$500 million to US$307 million, or 39%. As the equity of the deal was only US$13 million but had RWA of US$162 million, this could be sold to a hedge fund or other non-bank entity.

The AAA tranches would be considered nearly riskless and could be sold to investors directly, sold to structured investment vehicles (SIVs) or be insured by derivative product companies or monoline insurers. The AAA tranche might be kept in a trading book, and as stated earlier might attract very little capital as it would attract very little VaR. By selling or hedging the equity and the AAAs, the bank could reduce the RWA from US$500 million to US$61.5 million, nearly 88%. Income would also be reduced by selling the AAAs and the equity, but by a much smaller fraction.

Apart from reducing RWAs, banks were also motivated by the structuring and potential management fees which could be earned in precisely meeting investor needs via this type of financial engineering.

In order to reduce the RWA of the tranches between the AAA and the equity, banks would sell them to investors as they had much higher spreads than similarly rated corporate securities. Later in the cycle they might sell them into HG and Mezz CDOs (a full explanation of HG and Mezz levels in CDOs is given in the next section). This inevitably led to an explosion in CDOs which mirrored an explosion of systemic leverage.

Basel II addressed the potential regulatory arbitrage of simple two-tranche deals, and stipulated that the equity tranche required 100% capital. However, banks are always under pressure from the market to increase ROC. New securitisation tools were developed to effectively increase ROC by increasing leverage, which was easily facilitated by the risk-sensitive rules imposed under Basel II, and led to a golden era for banks.

Collateralised debt obligations (CDOs) became one of the banks' regulatory capital arbitrage products of choice. Widely distributed CDOs with thin tranches massively increased the amount of leverage possible.

In order, therefore, to understand fully how the family of STL risk indices can enable us to avoid the mistakes of the past, it's worth looking carefully at CDOs.

CDOs: splicing and reconstituting assets to reduce required capital

A collateralised debt obligation, or CDO, is a securitisation of virtually any type of debt, with typically 50 to 300 assets or reference credits. A **structured finance CDO** (SFCDO) is a CDO which itself buys ABS tranches from other securitisations. Some people occasionally see these as CDO 'squareds' as they are securitisations of assets issued by other securitisations. These SFCDOs then came in two general varieties:

1. high grade (HG SF CDO), which might be made up of A average-rated ABS tranches, and

2. mezzanine (Mezz SF CDO), which might be made up of BBB- (BBB minus) average rated ABS tranches.

As discussed earlier, these SFCDOs would often be invested in the tranches of other SFCDOs, further layering the risk.

In a Mezz SF CDO, an SPV might purchase a portfolio of ABSs which are on average rated BBB-, and then fund those assets via a new set of tranches. Under Basel II the underlying BBB- rated tranches would require risk weights of 100%. However, when rating agencies rated Mezz SF CDOs they usually assumed less than perfect correlation between the loss distributions of the various ABSs, due to the fact that underlying loans were originated in different geographical regions or belonged to different asset classes.

Structurers therefore found that they could get very high ratings for senior tranches of Mezz CDOs. Tables 4.2a and 4.2b show typical CDO structures, their pre-repackaging RWA and their post-repackaging RWA for typical Mezz and HG CDOs, respectively.

Table 4.2a: the typical CDO structure of a Mezz CDO with BBB- rated (BBB minus) debt, its pre-packaging RWA and its post-packaging RWA

Scenario A: Basel I

	Risk Weighting (%)	Size (%)	Amount (US$m)	RWA (US$m)
Pool of BBB-	100	100.00	1000	1000

Scenario B: Basel II

Tranche Rating	Risk Weighting (%)	Size (%)	Amount (US$m)	RWA (US$m)
AAA	7	80.00	800	56
AA	15	7.00	70	10.5
A	20	4.00	40	8
BBB	75	4.50	45	33.75
BB+	250	1.00	10	25
Sub-total non-equity		**96.50**	**965**	**133.25**
Equity	**1250**	**3.50**	**35**	**437.5**
Total		100	1000	570.75

Table 4.2b: the typical CDO structure of an HG CDO with A-rated debt, its pre-packaging RWA and its post-packaging RWAs

Scenario A: Basel I

	Risk Weighting (%)	Size (%)	Amount (US$m)	RWA (US$m)
Pool of A-	35	100.00	1000	350

Scenario B: Basel II

Tranche Rating	Risk Weighting (%)	Size (%)	Amount (US$m)	RWA (US$m)
AAA	7	85.00	850	59.5
AAA	12	7.00	70	8.4
AAA	12	4.00	40	4.8
AA	15	1.50	15	2.25
A	20	0.50	5	1
A-	35	0.20	2	0.7
BBB	75	1.00	10	7.5
Sub-total non-equity		**99.20**	**992**	**84.15**
Equity	**1250**	**0.8**	**8**	**100**
Total		100	1000	184.15

From Table 4.2a we can see that by repackaging mezzanine debt into a CDO, the sponsoring bank might be able to reduce the required capital by 43% without selling any assets.

The bank, however, would typically sell the equity to the CDO manager as it required very little cash. When the bank sold the equity tranche only, which for a Mezz SF CDO might only require US$35 million on a US$1 billion structure, the RWA would fall by nearly 87%, or from RWA of US$1 billion to US$133 million.

Similarly for an HG CDO, without selling any debt, the sponsoring bank would reduce RWA by 47%, and if they sold the equity tranche only, as was typical, they would reduce RWA by 76% or from US$350 million to US$84 million.

Securitisation vehicles that were built up between 1988 and 2007 allowed a reduction in capital usage for the same levels of risk – they allowed a build up of leverage.

Some CDO tranches were retained by banks without hedges, some were in trading books and attracted little capital due to their very low VaR. Many were funded by banks who bought CDS protection from insurance companies and monolines.

Further, it would be typical that the super senior tranche of these CDOs would be considered riskless from an economic standpoint, as they required far more subordination than was required for AAA.

Nonetheless, from the above example it can be seen that they might generate 70% of the non-equity RWA for a HG deal if they were retained in a banking book.

If they were kept in a trading book they would likely attract far less capital. As the banks were very interested in getting rid of these RWAs, they would buy protection from derivatives product companies, insurance companies and monoline insurers who considered these tranches riskless.

On top of all of this, the structuring bank would receive fees which would be paid out of the asset pool. These fees of, say, 50bps to 1% would go a long way to help selling the equity tranche.

Once the equity and senior AAA tranches were sold or hedged for a mezz deal, the measured RWA within the banking system would fall from US$1 billion to US$76 million, or 92.4%. For an HG deal, the RWA would fall from US$350 million to US$25.4 million, or 92.7%.

The initial securitisation of subprime loans, combined with hedging or selling the AAA and equity risks, reduced RWA by 90%. Then the other tranches could again be repackaged into CDOs, reducing RWA by a further 94% if again the equity and super senior portions of those deals were sold or hedged. This would leave a final reduction of 99% of the RWA. For the mezzanine tranches of CDOs which remained, they could be purchased by further CDOs, yet again repackaging them, and reducing required capital further.

Meanwhile, the actual level of risk within the financial system *remained the same*, and as we now know, most of the actual risk was still sitting with the banks that created these structures in the first place.

These are much like the investment trusts and utility holding companies we introduced earlier, which appear to have been a key element in causing the euphoric rise in the US stock market in the late 1920s, and likewise, in exacerbating the 1929 crash.

The result: an increase in systemic leverage

The net impact of this complex process of repackaging and distribution of risk was, of course, an increase in systemic leverage.

So, once more to recap:

1. Basel II in combination with the rapid leaps and bounds which took place in ratings, securitisation and credit derivative technology facilitated a massive increase in leverage by banks and within the overall financial system.

2. When we think about using the combination of repackaging subprime securitisations inside of CDOs, the capital savings are multiplied.

3. This capital savings also meant a massive amount of unused capital seeking assets, facilitating a drop in risk spreads, falling underwriting standards and excessive capital available support new lending.

4. In order to facilitate the massive new amount of lending, funding was required in addition to capital. Much of that funding was done via ABCP (asset-backed commercial paper), which was then sold to money market funds and institutional investors.

Of course, while this is interesting as a flaw in the Basel regulations, allowing a far smaller amount of required capital, it would really only have mattered if this methodology was being actively used. The problem was that the methodology *was* being actively used.

In 1990, the total US ABSs outstanding were US$40 billion. In 2000 it was US$854 billion, and by 2007, US$2499 billion. The market saw the huge opportunity to lever itself, within Basel guidelines, and believed in the rating agencies' assessments of risk. This is where it went wrong.

CDOs, which further reduced the need for regulatory capital vs. total outstanding claims, grew dramatically under Basel regulations, as shown in Table 4.3.

Table 4.3: Growth of CDO issuance under Basel regulations

CDO issuance	US$ (bn)
2004	157
2005	271
2006	520
2007	481
Total	1429

Total issuance then, from 2004 to 2007, was $1429 billion, facilitating a huge regulatory capital arbitrage.

Following the rules as they had been set out by regulators, banks were able to vastly increase their leverage and overall lending to consumers using securitisation. This is where we were in 2008. Since then the entire world has had to cope with the consequences.

The chief executive of Deutsche Bank, Josef Ackermann, said in March 2009 that the Basel framework for banking capital now needed "fundamental methodological adjustments" in light of the 2007-2009 financial crisis; banks must stop relying on narrow statistical systems to measure risk and regulators must adopt a "dynamic approach" in setting capital limits to force banks to build bigger buffers during good times.

> **" Banks must stop relying on narrow statistical systems to measure risk. "**

But what if a measure could be devised which restored the concept of leverage to its rightful place?

What if an indicator could be found that was statistically highly significant, and cut through the massive data and computer modelling which has confused and misled many of the brightest minds in the financial markets since Basel I and Basel II?

What if a measure could be utilised to give regulators and rating agencies a firmer grasp of the risks they were measuring?

All these wishes, we believe, are fulfilled by the family of STL risk indices.

The family of STL risk indices

What was lost through Basel I and Basel II for securitised assets was the concept of leverage. Since RWAs were not based on leverage, regulators stopped measuring it. Once the regulators stopped measuring leverage, they also in one sense stopped measuring sensitivity to unexpected losses. To see how this measurement might be applied to these new products we have to go back to simple banking and simple leverage.

For a simple portfolio where US$1 billion is lent, and for which the lending institution has US$100 million in capital, we can divide the total asset size by the capital base and see that we are ten times levered. This is important and can be looked at in many ways. First, any losses up to 10% are covered by capital and the institution remains solvent.

Another way of looking at this might be to ask, if we are wrong about our belief concerning the underlying loss distribution, how sensitive are we to that assumption? For that, we can

> **❝** When regulators stopped measuring leverage they also stopped measuring sensitivity to unexpected losses. **❞**

see that we are levered ten times and therefore for every .01% that our actual loss distribution is worse than what we expected, we will lose ten times .01%, or 0.10%. For readers who are mathematicians, this is the first derivative of the value of our capital with respect to losses in the asset portfolio. This is an incredibly useful measure for stress testing and is a measure of how confident we must be to remain levered to this degree. It allows you to directly measure your sensitivity to errors in assumptions about the loss distribution.

The concept of leverage within ABS has been addressed in many ways, but never in the way in which STL(0) allows.

Defining simple tranche leverage STL(0) and see-through leverage STL(X) for securitisation structures

For any securitisation structure, the capital structure defines the subordination and seniority of each tranche or slice of capital. Each tranche may have some amount of subordination under it and each tranche may be itself subordinate to other more senior tranches. The amount of subordination, as well as the amount of debt senior to a tranche in the capital structure, may be represented as a percentage of the whole capital structure. The **width** of a tranche may be defined as the percentage of capital represented by a tranche itself.

We can now define simple tranche leverage as the width of a tranche plus the total debt senior to that tranche, divided by the width of that same tranche.

```
Simple tranche leverage, or STL(0)  =  (100% - tranche attachment %)
                                        _____
                                        (tranche detachment - tranche
                                                  attachment)
```

We will represent simple tranche leverage with the symbol STL(0). Note that STL(0) ignores any specific information about the assets which are purchased by the capital. One will notice that for an equity tranche, or a tranche with no subordination, this is simply what we would normally refer to as its leverage. In a sense we are extending that well-known metric to now include that measure for every tranche.

In order to more effectively capture the risk of the structure we also need to look at the underlying assets the capital purchases. In the case of a CDO, a securitisation may purchase pieces of other securitisations. The assets purchased by the outer securitisation may themselves have an STL(0) as above.

In this way, we can now define see-through leverage level 1 or STL(1) as STL(0) for the outer capital structure multiplied by the average STL(0) for the assets purchased. So STL(0) capital structure times STL(0) assets equals STL(1).

As in a CDO there may be several layers of securitisations involved. We can define STL(X) for any number (X) depending on the number of securitisation layers we need to see through. See-through leverage then may be defined as

STL(X) where X reaches the bottom floor – where we see loans or bonds which themselves are not a securitisation.

STL(X) is a mathematical approximation of a tranche's sensitivity to errors in underlying loss assumptions at the point where losses first touch that tranche.

Then STL(X), which measures the lender's leverage, can also be enhanced to include borrower leverage. For example, we define ESTL(X) as STL(X) multiplied by the leverage of the ultimate borrower (this can be surmised from the loan-to-value ratios (LTVs) of mortgages). Then we have created an index which contains the layering of risk implied by both the borrowers and lenders.

A schematic showing how STL is calculated can be seen in Figure 4.1.

Figure 4.1: A schematic showing how the algorithm to calculate STL operates

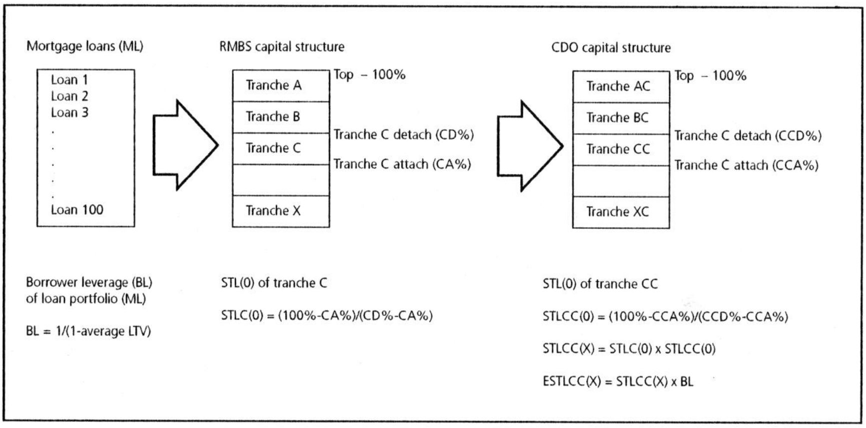

Let's walk through some examples.

Example A

If there is a typical subprime securitisation, a BBB+ rated tranche might have subordination of 5% and might be itself 1.5% wide, and therefore will be supporting 93.5% of the liabilities above it. Then we can calculate STL(0) as 93.5 / 1.5 or 62.3 times levered. Let's assume a mezz CDO is filled primarily with these securities. Then if we look at the super senior tranche of a mezz ABS CDO, which would get nearly zero capital allocated to it if it was hedged with an insurance company, that AAA tranche would have an STL(0) of 1 times the underlying asset STL(0) of 62.3, which would make STL(X) 62.3, which means the security is 62.3 times levered.

This is very similar to the amount of leverage achieved by LTCM, the infamous hedge fund whose insolvency rocked the financial system in 1998. If it was not hedged under Basel II it would need 7% times 8% or 56bps of capital in a regulated bank. *Required capital of 56bps means the regulated bank could lever itself 100% / .56% or 178.5 times with these 62.3 times levered assets, achieving a see-through leverage of 178.5 times 62.3, or over 11,120 times.*

Example B

The junior AAA tranche of an HG ABS CDO might have 5% subordination and be 3% thick. This alone then has an STL(0) of 95 / 3, or 31.6. In addition these deals would be in large part comprised of underlying ABS assets with STL(0) of 54. The combined STL(X) for this junior AAA tranche might then be 31.6 times 54, or 1706.

Basel II, under IRB, required 12% times 8%, or 96bps, in capital for this 1706 times levered asset. While the asset might have no losses as long as the underlying asset pool had less than 7% losses (the typical subordination for A-rated subprime assets), once they reached 7% losses the extreme STL(X) would wipe out the investment almost immediately. The STL(X) that might be achieved by a bank would then again be 100% / 0.96%, or 104.1 times 1706, which is equal to 177,594 times levered.

In simple terms, what if the rating agency was wrong about its estimate for the underlying losses of the subprime pools? How sensitive is the junior AAA-rated HG ABS CDO to those errors in judgment?

An STL(X) of 1706 means that if losses were far greater than expected, and the subordination was for some reason wiped out below all the A-rated ABS securities in a CDO, a 0.01% additional loss would cause a loss of 17.06% of the AAA-rated junior tranche. A 0.06% error in the loss distribution at that level wipes out your entire investment, because a 0.06% loss in the underlying times 1706 is equal to a 102% loss overall. In this example, *an additional 0.06% loss in the underlying loan assets, once subordination has been wiped out, could cause a 100% loss in the CDO tranche, but only 0.96% of capital is required under Basel II.* Many new and innovative structures of the past 20 years, since the advent of Basel I, can be looked at this way.

The amount of capital a bank needs should be enough to cover unexpected losses. By using RWAs that were based on the ratings of agencies, the Basel rules do not have a reliable measure of unexpected losses, but are instead measuring expected losses. Relying mainly on agency ratings eliminates leverage as a concept for securitisation structures, and therefore does not measure the sensitivity of an asset to errors in the assumptions of underlying loss distributions. The family of STL indices measures leverage – one measure of the sensitivity to errors in loss distribution estimates – and allows another view of 'unexpected' losses. STL indices should therefore be used as a measure of riskiness to determine required capital.

Next we will show in a simple theoretical example how STL is a true measure of the sensitivity of a tranched security to changes in the loss distribution. STL truly measures sensitivity to unexpected losses.

A theoretical STL example for explanatory purposes

In this section we will present a theoretical example to explain in the simplest possible terms the concepts behind ratings and STL(0) for a securitised pool of assets. To this end we will examine two different possible loss distributions for a portfolio of securitised loans, and will examine the effects of the change from one loss distribution to another for two different tranches of securities which absorb different parts of those losses.

Figure 4.2: a frequency chart showing two alternative future loss distributions for a class of loans

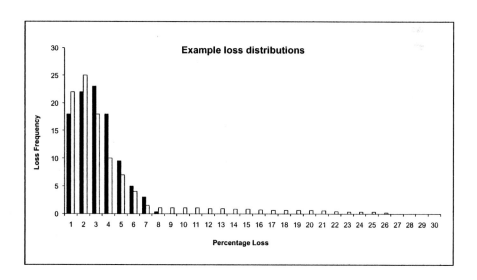

In general the losses tend to be low and tightly distributed around the average losses. As you can see in Figure 4.2 the loss distribution in black has a higher frequency of smaller losses, while the white distribution has a wider distribution of losses and in general a higher frequency of larger losses. Let's call the black distribution *loss distribution A* and the white distribution *loss distribution B*.

Next let's examine the effects of these loss distributions on two different potential investments from a capital structure funding these assets. Let's look at a 7% to 8% tranche (one which absorbs losses beginning at 7% up to 8%) and a 7% to 100% tranche. Table 4.4 summarises the results of certain tests for these assets using the above loss distributions.

Table 4.4: A summary of the effects of using the loss distributions in Figure 4.2

Asset	Loss distribution A	Loss distribution B	STL(0)
Expected loss portfolio	2.05%	2.87%	NA
Expected loss 7%-8%	0.0050%	11.5000%	93
Expected loss 7%-100%	0.0001%	0.1237%	1

As can be seen, the average or expected losses of the portfolio are 2.05% under loss distribution A and 2.87% under loss distribution B. In order for there to be any losses to a 7% to 8% tranche or a 7% to 100% tranche, there must be losses far larger than the expected ones. These are generally known as 'unexpected losses' of the loan pool.

As it turns out, loss distribution A is very unlikely to experience a loss of greater than 7% and therefore the 7% to 8% and the 7% to 100% tranches experience just 0.005% loss and 0.0001% loss respectively. Therefore the unexpected losses of the portfolio create only miniscule expected losses to these tranches. It is likely that both securities might be AAA-rated under these assumptions and the 7% to 8% tranche might only require 96bps of capital, and the 7% to 100% might require only 56bps of capital, under Basel II.

On the other hand things change dramatically if we examine the impact of loss distribution B. Now the expected loss of the loan pool is 2.87%, really only a very small change. Still, in order to experience any loss for either of our tranches, the pool must experience losses far greater than the average, or they must experience unexpected losses. However, the expected losses to the 7% to 8% tranche now explode; the expected loss of the tranche is over 11.5% – an extremely risky security. On the other hand the 7% to 100% tranche remains a creditworthy investment, experiencing only 12.37bps in expected losses.

From all of this we see that while we have only a 0.8% change in the expected loss of the portfolio of loans[46] the effects of that change, in conjunction with a change in the dispersion of those losses, can dramatically impact the value of a high STL(0) security.

While the low, or STL(0) = 1, security remains a fairly stable investment under both loss distributions, and in fact a capital requirement of 56bps covers the expected losses under either loss distribution, that is not the case for the STL(0) = 93 security. This security is fine with a 96bps capital requirement if we have the distribution right. However, if we have the distribution wrong, the required capital needs to be far larger, arguably much more than 11.5%, or more than 11 times greater. In fact, if we assume capital should cover any loss event occurring once in ten years, we need 100% capital for this investment rather than 96bps or 100 times more capital.

What this example shows

The above example shows how the concepts of expected loss of a loan portfolio, expected losses of a tranche and unexpected losses relate. It also shows how STL(0) is an important measure of sensitivity to errors in predicted loss distributions, an important indicator of the stability of an investment and an important indicator of likely stability of capital requirements under Basel II.

Now that we have shown a worked theoretical example, we will next look at how well STL(X) would have done in practice. We will show that STL(X) would have, in retrospect, predicted that what became known as toxic AAA securities were very risky. STL(X) would have indicated to regulators that there was extreme systemic risk throughout the banking system, before the crisis occurred.

---

[46] 2.87% (expected loss of distribution B) minus 2.05% (expected loss of distribution A) = 0.82%.

STL as a barometer of risk in practice

How well does the STL family of risk indices predict riskiness in practice?

In order to evaluate STL's usefulness as an investment tool, we can apply two types of tests:

1. Does STL explain retrospectively the downgrades that have occurred in ABS assets, and therefore the massive increase in required capital which banks now seek?

To this end, we regressed the natural log of the STL(X) of over 300 different ABS securities issued in 2006 and 2007 against the current ratings for those securities. As this was done in 2009, the current ratings should much better reflect their actual risks. We tested a very wide set of assets: credit cards, auto loans, prime **residential mortgage-backed securities** (RMBSs), subprime RMBSs, alternative a-paper (alt a) loans, CDOs, CSOs, etc. We ignored the underlying asset class and all waterfall features and instead just looked at rating and estimated STL(X). We discovered that the natural log of STL(X) (as it stands today, and as it stood on the day the securities were issued) explains 43% of the variation in the ratings of these securities. The t-statistic for the natural log of STL(X) was 14.46, highly statistically significant. If we instead use the original ratings of these securities to try to explain the current ratings we find they explain just 10% of the variation for this group of securities.

We also created another index for these same securities, whereby we multiplied the STL(X) by the leverage of the borrowers for those securities which have LTVs, or ESTL(X). When we regressed the natural log of this index against the current ratings we found it explained 54% of the variation, with a t-stat of more than 18. Next we segregated out just the AAA-rated securities and found similar results, although slightly lower. The original ratings of the AAA-rated securities alone explain none of the current variation in those ratings. This risk estimation process is extremely simple and quick, and it tells you which AAA ratings are likely toxic and which are not.

2. Does STL explain the change in value of AAA assets of home equity loans?

We looked at a single asset class of home equity loan securities originally rated AAA. We then regressed the STL(X) vs. the current market price and found we could explain 70% of the price variation, completely ignoring geography, servicer, originator, etc. Again, this simple, easy to estimate measure of leverage gives an indication as to which AAA-rated securities are toxic and which are not.

The advent of Basel I and Basel II caused a massive increase in issuance of innovative new securitisation structures which reduced the necessary regulatory capital required against a given asset pool. Basel II essentially threw out the notion of leverage for ABSs. As a new definition of leverage, STL(X) can be used to explain:

- How a massive asset bubble was allowed to be created.

- How banks were able to massively reduce the capital needed against those pools.

- How to tell the difference between potentially toxic AAA-rated assets and safer AAA assets.

Armed with this tool the regulators and rating agencies should measure STL(X) and use it to consider whether assets with high STL(X) should be rated AAA and whether we should have a higher required minimum capital for high STL(X) assets.

In the next chapter we will examine in detail how STL(X) can help regulators and rating agencies and give some concrete examples of how STL(X) can offer a measure of the utmost utility in today's financial markets in a fraction of the time normally spent on ratings-based models.

5

How STL Should Be Used In Practice By Investors, Regulators And Rating Agencies

Chapter summary

- STL is an easy to understand, easy to calculate, powerful risk measurement tool.

- In this chapter we will re-introduce STL in another intuitive way, and show how it differs from other more common references to leverage for structured credit products.

- We will give a number of examples of how to calculate STL across different asset types – including automobile loans, credit cards and home equity loans – and it will become clearer why certain structures blew up first and why some have not blown up at all.

- We will also introduce yet another way to think about STL, which will explain why even banks who hedged themselves found they accrued large losses.

- VaR type models are flawed for highly engineered and regulatory capital optimised structured credit products such as CDOs and therefore we explore why using VaR as a measure of required capital for these products can be quite dangerous and pro-cyclical.

- All of this, of course, leads towards the need for a new set of regulatory capital rules, which will direct us to Chapter Six: Towards a Basel III.

Note: As mentioned earlier, in the case of a structure with just one layer, which is the typical example used in this book, STL = STL(0) = STL(X), so the terms are interchangeable.

STL(X) is really see-through leverage!

In spite of the rules and requirements of Basel I, the accord fell short of appropriately measuring and controlling a key risk: leverage. Through the use of derivatives and securitisation, any bank can create any nominal balance-sheet leverage multiple any regulator or investor wants to see for any risk profile the bank wishes to have. Therefore, the nominal measure of leverage becomes irrelevant.

We will now take a look at two examples of this.

Example A

Suppose you are a bank and you want to have a balance sheet leveraged 50 times, but your regulator wants you to be at most ten times leveraged using their nominal measure of leverage; you can accomplish this easily. Say you have US$100 in capital and have US$900 in deposits. Take the underlying asset you want to invest in, say a corporate bond, and call your favourite credit structuring bank. Ask if you can buy a levered **credit-linked note** (CLN) referencing that corporate credit levered five times. That structuring bank will look and see whether that corporate bond has an active market and, even better, will see whether there is an active CDS market for that reference name. They will look at the rating and see how liquid or actively traded that CDS is and what its worst or highest ever day-to-day volatility has been. In addition they will probably also look at the highest daily volatility of any CDS or security that has a similar rating and industry profile.

If they are able to convince themselves that the risk of any one-day movement in the mark to market of that CDS will never imply more than a 5% movement in the underlying bond, then they may, for a fee, be very happy to take on the gap risk of a single day movement of 20%.[47]

They can then structure a market risk trigger whereby you, the investor, can put up US$1000 to buy a CLN which references US$5000 of the corporate bond, with a market trigger where the structuring bank gets to sell or de-lever the structure if the bond falls in price by, say, 10% or more.

You, the investor, will get a CLN spread of five times the normal credit spread minus the gap fee taken by the structuring bank. If the market moves against you it is very easy to imagine that you will have a complete loss of your investment, the structuring bank will earn its fee and you took the risk you wished to take to earn your high income.

Meanwhile, you're making a US$1000 investment, using US$100 in capital, which references US$5000 in bonds. Of course, if everything goes well, you would have earned a very high return.

Using the current technology of derivatives and securitisation via this simple market-based trigger CLN, you appear to be only ten times levered. On the other hand, if we had measured the leverage using STL(X), we would have

---

[47] In general, in our opinion, this bank may be making a key conceptual error in this analysis, but that discussion is not relevant to this book.

calculated your investment as 50 times levered. It is obvious then that STL(X) better reveals the real risk of leverage.

Example B

Here is a further example to show how STL is just a true measure of traditional leverage for securitisations.

Let's say you buy a 3% to 6% tranche of a securitised pool of assets. We can easily calculate the STL for this:

Your capital investment is 3% (6% - 3%) and there is 97% of the capital structure above your attachment point. So:

$$\frac{97\%}{3\%} = 32.3, \text{ or } 32.3 \text{ times STL.}$$

How could this same risk profile be achieved via traditional finance?

Say you find a traditional bank that likes the safety of the loans being securitised. Assume they think there is essentially no chance this pool of loans will suffer a loss of greater than 3% under any circumstances. Then you might agree to the following deal with them. You could agree that you will put up 3% in cash, and you will buy the 3% to 100% portion of the securitised pool of assets.

In other words you will get full repayment as long as losses remain below 3% and for any losses above 3% your investment takes the hit. As the traditional lending bank believes there is no chance of any losses above 3% they may be very happy to lend you the 94% you need (in addition to your 3% cash) to buy the entire 3% to 100% tranche for some reasonable interest rate where the bank earns a comfortable spread or fee.

The bank might also agree that this will be a *non-recourse* transaction, i.e. they will take the tranche investment as their only collateral against the loan. This means that even if actual losses far exceed 3% and the lending bank will not get fully repaid from the asset itself, they cannot come back to you, the borrower, and ask for the rest.

Think about the exposure that has been created. You have bought a 3% to 100% tranche by using 3% cash and you borrowed the rest, with no recourse other than to the tranche itself. You get returns and risk economically equivalent to the 3% to 6% tranche. The traditional measure of leverage for this would be 97% / 3% = 32.3 times leverage. So, again, see-through leverage can be thought of as the traditional measure of leverage applied to securitisation products, or for that matter all new structured-credit products.

Next we will examine a number of other concrete examples. We will begin with simpler, less risky securities and then follow with riskier, more complex examples, until finally we finish with what we now know are the most risky types of securities: ABS CDOs.

Examples of securitisations

Stylised auto loan securitisation

Today nearly every type of debt can be securitised, and in particular one of the main sources of financing consumer debt is via securitisation.

The first auto loan securitisations were completed in 1985, and ever since they have been a major portion of the ABS market. According to SIFMA, US auto-loan backed ABSs peaked at US$234.5 billion in 2003 and stood at US$135.9 billion at the end of Q4 2009.[48]

A customer goes to a dealer having decided it is time to buy a new car. The finance company asks the customer to fill out the paperwork and for a small deposit they get to buy a new car, borrowing the rest from the finance company. The customer needs to make their monthly payments or the car will be repossessed. The finance company then needs to borrow the money from someone else. One way they can do that is by taking a large pool of similar auto loans made to creditworthy individuals, selling them into a special purpose vehicle (SPV) and then that SPV can sell bonds to investors which fund the loan portfolio. These bonds will be configured so that their coupon, maturity, rating, etc, will match the needs and risk appetites of the target investors. As can be seen from the stylised example in Table 5.1, a pool of auto loans may be turned into mainly AAA-rated bonds, which are highly sought-after by conservative, safety-minded investors. Here's how the tranche structure might look.

---

[48] Figures from SIFMA.

Table 5.1: how an auto loan tranche structure might look

Tranche	Size(000s)	Subordination or Attachment	Detachment	Width	Original Rating	STL
A	150,000	72.58%	100.00%	27.42%	A1+	1.0
B	50,000	63.44%	72.58%	9.14%	AAA	4.0
C	300,000	8.59%	63.44%	54.84%	AAA	1.7
D	25,000	4.02%	8.59%	4.57%	A	21.0
E	8000	2.56%	4.02%	1.46%	BBB	66.6
F	4000	1.83%	2.56%	0.73%	BB	134.3
G	4000	1.10%	1.83%	0.73%	B	135.3
Equity	6000	0.00%	1.10%	1.10%	Not Rated	91.2
Total	547,000					

While neither the borrower nor the lender may consider the borrowers of this money to buy these cars as AAA or A1+ credit risks, 91% of the capital structure is rated AAA or A1+. Likewise, probably none of the individual borrowers are thought to be so bad that they would be considered purely speculative, unrateable equity.

What has happened?

As was shown in chapter two, the assumption of less-than-perfect correlation between defaults of borrowers means that the default risk in a portfolio gets concentrated around the expected loss of the portfolio. Also, the excess spread due to individual borrowers having to pay more than the individual expected loss they generate means more cash for subordination protection. This means the predicted loss distribution is small and concentrated. In addition we should take note of the STL for each tranche. The top tranche has an STL of 1, the least risky. There are two other AAA-rated tranches, which fall lower in the capital structure, which have higher STLs and are riskier.

It is also interesting to note that the STL of tranche C is lower than that of tranche B. As tranche C is subordinate to tranche B and would be wiped out before tranche B if excess losses were to occur, and therefore is riskier, we see that while STL is an important measure, it cannot be used in isolation. STL is just one measure of riskiness. Later on we will see examples of AAA-rated assets with very high STLs.

Now let's look at something else that is a daily feature of our lives: credit cards.

Credit card securitisation

When a customer borrows money from an auto finance company, that company then needs to borrow the money from somewhere else (very possibly indirectly from your money market account). The process is the same with a credit card company – they must borrow money to make the payments to the retailer, restaurant or whatever store the credit card holder bought something from when they charged something to their card and decided to wait a month or two before fully paying the credit card company back. Much of that borrowing is done via credit card ABS.

As can be seen from the stylised example in Table 5.2, 86.54% of the liabilities issued by a pool of credit card debt may be considered AAA. By securitising credit card debt, most of it can be converted into highly rated bonds for conservative investors. The first public credit card ABS deals were completed in 1987 and ever since then it has represented one of the largest segments of the ABS market. According to SIFMA, US credit card ABS outstanding peaked at US$401.9 billion in 2003, and in Q4 2009 stood at US$292 billion.

It is interesting to note that both credit card and auto ABS peaked in 2003. Thereafter, as evidenced by the rapid growth in home equity ABS, many households began to use home mortgages as a cheaper and more tax efficient way of borrowing. They used mortgages in order to pay back credit card debt and finance consumption in general. Table 5.2 provides an example of a credit card ABS tranche liability structure.

Again, here we can turn a normal everyday individual's credit card payments into AAA-rated securities using the magic of low-correlation assumptions, excess spread, and tranching. We also see an AAA-rated security with an STL of 1, as the security itself does not exhibit any leverage. On the other hand the lower-rated securities have far higher STLs and higher expected losses due to the lesser protection or subordination afforded them in this structure.

Table 5.2: an example of a credit card ABS tranche liability structure

Tranche	Size (000s)	Subordination or Attachment	Detachment	Width	Original Rating	STL
A	450,000	13.46%	100.00%	86.54%	AAA	1.0
B	30,000	7.69%	13.46%	5.77%	A	16.0
C	40,000	0.00%	7.69%	7.69%	BBB	13.0
Total	**520,000**					

Student loan securitisation

Paying for university for a single child, never mind multiple children, can be a huge task for any family in America. A university education costs thousands of dollars, and many families do not have that much liquidity on hand even if they have saved for years to help support their child's or childrens' education.

In order to help alleviate this problem and allow a wide portion of the American population to go to college, the US Department of Education supports various student loan programmes which are then guaranteed by the US Department of Education under most circumstances. These student loans are then packaged so that they can be securitised and sold to investors. The vast majority of the assets are deemed AAA, making them highly appealing to safety-minded bond investors.

Once again we see loans being turned into highly-rated securities using the magic of securitisation and the rating agencies' assumptions. We also see that there are three sets of securities all with different levels of subordination or protection. While all three AAA-rated tranches have the same ratings agency label, STL shows some small differentiation in their levels of risk. Here tranche C has a higher STL than tranche A, reflecting the greater potential risk of the higher STL rating.

Table 5.3: an example of a student loan tranche structure

Tranche	Size (000s)	Subordination or Attachment	Detachment	Width	Original Rating	STL
A	450,000	13.46%	100.00%	86.54%	AAA	1.0
B	225,000	47.47%	64.98%	17.51%	AAA	3.0
C	280,000	25.68%	47.47%	21.79%	AAA	3.4
D	300,000	2.33%	25.68%	23.35%	A+	4.2
E	30,000	0	2.33%	2.33%	Not rated	42.8
Total	520,000					

Home equity ABS

Home equity loans and subprime mortgages make up a huge category of loans within the world of securitisation. Home equity loans were originally loans to homeowners wanting to make home improvements facilitated by dipping into the equity available in their homes. Subprime mortgages are generally those made to subprime borrowers, or those borrowers with low FICO scores (the the most widely used type of credit scores in the US). Home equity ABS refers to securitisations which could contain one, the other or both types of loans. In the United States, unlike most debt, residential mortgages are tax-deductible and therefore tend to be by far the cheapest form of debt available.

A borrower might be deemed subprime for one of many reasons. The amount of deposit put down on the house might be very low, the borrower might have missed a number of payments on previous loans or the borrower may be too highly leveraged overall in regards to debt vs. total income. Due to their riskier profile, home equity loans and subprime mortgages require much higher interest payments. Nonetheless, since house prices in the United States rose consistently for many years, a house was always considered a good personal investment. In essence the US government, through mortgage interest deductibility, subsidised the US housing market in order to encourage home ownership. Many a US president has bragged about the high rate of home ownership in the US as a sign of prosperity.

Given the tax deductibility of home loans and the consistently rising prices of homes historically, individuals generally buy a house not only as a place to live but as a key to their future financial security. If a home can be bought with 10% down, or with ten times leverage, a 10% increase in the value of that house means a 100% return on investment in addition to a place to live. In recent years – during the housing bubble of the early 21st century – rising house prices also meant that some home owners began to rely on their homes not only as good investments for the future, but as vehicles to fund current spending.

Many home buyers ended up buying the largest house possible on their income, using the maximum leverage. This was a quite rational approach to maximising net worth as long as house prices kept rising. However, many of those borrowers found that they had stretched themselves too thinly and were not willing or able to make the sacrifices necessary to live on their incomes alone. So, in many cases, their home became their ATM machine.

> **"Once house prices fell some people had no resource to generate cash to pay off their debts. This led to foreclosures across the country."**

A homeowner would find themselves unable to pay off their expensive credit card debt because they had spent more than their current income. They would then look and see that the home they had purchased last year had risen in value. A bank or mortgage company would offer to consolidate their debt and lower their borrowing costs. So the bank would issue a new mortgage for a larger size which was possible because the price of the house had risen, and the bank would use the cash generated by the higher mortgage to pay off the expensive credit card debt.

For the borrower this was terrific because, as we have seen, they were able to replace expensive credit card debt with cheap tax-deductible debt and start all over again. If interest rates had dropped in the meantime, it might also be that the larger loan could be accomplished with no increase in monthly payments.

As time went on, mortgage companies also developed new types of loans, floating rate loans with low teaser rates, or ones that allowed payment deferrals which would push payments from today to tomorrow. As long as house prices rose, this strategy worked. However, once house prices fell, and with them the value of the equity in houses, people had no other recourse to generate cash to pay off their debts. The home as ATM was closed. This then led to foreclosures and financial ruin across the US.

Subprime and Alt-A mortgages

As an important side note to this example, we should address the issue of subprime mortgage and Alt-A mortgage delinquencies and defaults which clearly were the instigating factor in the 2007-2009 crisis. As clearly stated in Federal Reserve research, the main factor behind the huge increase in defaults by these borrowers was the same factor behind the riskiness of ABS; leverage.

As stated in one paper:

> Slackened underwriting standards – manifested most dramatically by lenders allowing borrowers to forgo down payments entirely – combined with stagnant to falling house prices in many parts of the country appear to be the most immediate contributors to the rise in mortgage defaults. Because down payments were so small when house prices declined, many borrowers had little or no equity in their properties and thus little incentive to repay their mortgages.[49]

A 10% down payment is a loan with ten times leverage. A 5% down payment is a loan with 20 times leverage.

A mortgage with no equity means infinite leverage. As we stated in chapter four, if we multiply the average leverage of mortgage borrowers within a pool by the STL or leverage of the lenders, the statistical significance of predicting the current ratings of MBS and CMBS securities increases.

As can be seen in the stylised example in Table 5.4, while the borrowers were clearly below prime due to excess leverage or poor payment history, the pool of loans could be structured into different tranches with mainly AAA-rated bonds. This meant that highly safety-conscious investors could happily gorge themselves on these bonds, relying on the opinions of rating agencies.

With regard to STL we see something new here. We see an AAA-rated security with an STL of 28.2, while the highest STL we had seen previously on an AAA-rated security was 4.

An STL of 28.2 means this is a highly levered security and a single basis point loss in the underlying loan portfolio at the point when no subordination is left will cause a 28bps loss in this AAA-rated investment. This security is much more susceptible to errors in the ratings-agency model assumptions.

---

[49] Mayer, Pence, Sherlund, 'The Rise in Mortgage Defaults', Finance and Economics Discussion Series, Divisions of Research & Statistics and Monetary Affairs, Federal Reserve Board, Washington DC, 2008-59, p. 23.

Interestingly, this is a subprime mortgage example, and we now know that this was a far riskier asset class than credit cards, auto loans or student loans.

Table 5.4: a home equity tranche structure – subprime RMBS example

Tranche	Size (000s)	Subordination or Attachment	Detachment	Width	Original Rating	STL
A	300,000	66.37%	100.00%	33.63%	AAA	1.0
B	300,000	32.74%	66.37%	33.63%	AAA	2.0
C	80,000	23.77%	32.74%	8.97%	AAA	8.5
D	25,000	20.96%	23.77%	2.80%	AAA	28.2
E	30,000	17.60%	20.96%	3.36%	AA+	24.5
F	30,000	14.24%	17.60%	3.36%	AA+	25.5
G	20,000	12.00%	14.24%	2.24%	AA	39.3
H	15,000	10.31%	12.00%	1.68%	AA-	53.3
I	15,000	8.63%	10.31%	1.68%	A+	54.3
J	14,000	7.06%	8.63%	1.57%	A	59.2
K	12,000	5.72%	7.06%	1.35%	A-	70.1
L	10,000	4.60%	5.72%	1.12%	BBB+	85.1
M	10,000	3.48%	4.60%	1.12%	BBB	86.1
N	7000	2.69%	3.48%	0.78%	BBB	124.0
O	7000	1.91%	2.69%	0.78%	BBB-	125.0
P	3000	1.57%	1.91%	0.34%	BB+	292.7
Q	14,000	0.00%	1.57%	1.57%	Not Rated	63.7
Total	892,000					

Now let's examine some corporate examples starting with corporate leveraged loans.

Collateralised loan obligation (CLO)

One of the prime drivers of asset prices are private equity firms who search the markets for undervalued companies. The reasons for under-valuations often include inefficient operations, unrelated non-core activities which have poor return on capital, or just financing structures which are deemed too conservative. Private equity firms then purchase these underperforming companies by putting up a small amount of capital and levering that capital with what are known as leveraged loans. Leveraged loans are loans with far higher than normal leverage and are therefore riskier and typically rated at around BB. As can be seen in the following example, by assuming low correlation among the loans, while the underlying assets may be BB, the bulk of the bonds issued from a vehicle backed by these loans can be rated AAA by rating agencies, making them highly appealing to more conservative investors.

Table 5.5: an example of a CLO tranche structure

Tranche	Size (000s)	Subordination or Attachment	Detachment	Width	Original Rating	STL
A	300,000	25.00%	100.00%	75.00%	AAA	1
B	40,000	15.00%	25.00%	10.00%	A	9
C	20,000	10.00%	15.00%	5.00%	BBB-	18
D	40,000	0.00%	10.00%	10.00%	Equity	10
Total	400,000					

Collateralised synthetic obligation (CSO) or corporate single tranche CDO (STCDO)

In a corporate single tranche CDO, a portfolio of typically 100 or more corporate debt obligations are referenced. As with any credit derivative transaction, the terms include a number of credit events in the documentation, such as failure to pay or bankruptcy, which determine a default event.

In the case of a credit event for a reference asset, if it is determined an event of default has occurred, a recovery rate must be decided in order to calculate what loss is incurred on the portfolio from the event of default. Once a loss amount is calculated, the equivalent amount of subordination from such a deal is removed and no more cash flows will be paid to investors below that level ever again. If a tranche is untouched by any losses, it continues to receive payments as normal.

For example, assume an investment in a 3% to 6% tranche of a 100-name corporate portfolio. For simplicity every event of default has a 50% recovery rate (or in other words, also a 50% loss rate given default). If one default occurs it incurs a loss of just 0.5% on the portfolio and the 3% to 6% tranche is unaffected. If there are six defaults, that constitutes a 3% (or 0.5% x 6) loss for the portfolio, and hence the 3% to 6% tranche is still unaffected, but now has no subordination or protection from defaults left. Everything up to 3% is wiped out. Every event of default thereafter begins to erode the interest and principal payments to the 3% to 6% tranche investor. If there are 12 events of default, there is a total portfolio loss of 6% and therefore the 3% to 6% tranche is fully wiped out and this tranche experiences a complete loss of principal.

The reference portfolios for these deals are typically highly diversified corporate portfolios consisting of average BBB or BBB+ credits.

There are also STCDO deals with so-called *short buckets*. In these deals the manager might have the ability to also buy protection on certain names the manager feels may default. In the case of a default of a name where the manager has bought protection, subordination is increased, and may bring back to life tranches which had been previously wiped out.

In general, these deals can have a managed pool of reference credits which are changed periodically by a manager, or can be static where they never change over the life of the deal. They can also be either funded or unfunded. In a funded case, a bank could issue a CDO whose payoff is defined in line with the payoff of the STCDO.

Alternatively a credit-linked note (CLN) could be issued by an SPV which sells STCDO protection to a counterparty such as a dealer bank and invests in a charged asset – typically a highly-rated security – which would need to be liquidated in the case of losses or maturity of the note.

Table 5.6: a stylised example of an STL calculated for an AAA STCDO or CSO

Tranche	Size (000s)	Subordination or Attachment	Detachment	Width	Original Rating	STL
A	100,000	7.50%	8.50%	1.00%	AAA	92.5

Note what we see here. The STL of this AAA CSO tranche is extremely high in comparison to the STLs of the AAA-rated credit cards or the AAA-rated auto deals we saw earlier. This means that this AAA-rated asset is potentially far more sensitive to errors in the modelling of the loss distributions. If the underlying probabilities of default are wrong or if the correlation assumptions are wrong, these assets may be riskier than implied by the AAA rating.

The leveraged exposure is over 90 times to already levered companies, but it is rated AAA, which means that under Basel II very little capital is needed to support this highly model-dependent asset.

In addition, this asset may also be eligible for money market investments in some jurisdictions. The AAA rating of this asset does not tell you the complete story. The high STL warns you this is a riskier security. A 1% increase in losses at the point where no subordination is left more than wipes out this investment.

High-grade ABS CDO

The idea behind ABS CDOs is to take the lower rated (mainly non-AAA), higher-spread bonds issued by asset-backed and mortgage-backed securities and convert them into mostly AAA-rated securities with high yields making them very attractive to conservative investors.

This typically presents opportunities for arbitrage deals. One can buy assets with high-spread coupons and then repackage them together into a CDO to take full advantage of their diversification; that CDO can then issue, on average, higher-rated liabilities and sell them with a lower average spread. The resulting arbitrage spread can be extracted by the arranger as a fee, or it can be paid as excess spread to the holders of the equity tranche.

These types of deals are also known as re-securitisations. This is because they take existing asset-backed securities (tranches) and then put them into another securitisation where the portfolio of tranches is tranched once again.

This means that the calculation of STL is a two-step process. First, calculate the average STL(X) or leverage of the underlying ABS asset pool. We do this in the following stylised example by presenting the average STLs for a number of asset types.

Once the STL(X) for the asset pool is found then calculate the STL(0) for the specific tranche in the CDO structure. By multiplying the asset STL(X) by the STL(0) of the CDO structure we get what we call *STL(X)* or *see-through leverage for the entire structure.*

Table 5.7 shows what the asset composition of a high-grade (HG) ABS CDO might look like. As you can see there are many asset types of different ratings, ensuring a high level of diversity and a high average rating. What you will also notice is that these assets themselves are already levered securities.

The table shows what percentage each asset class may be of the entire portfolio, an estimated STL(X) for each class, and then, by multiplying the two, a contribution to an estimated STL(X) for the portfolio. As you can see, in this stylised case the asset pool itself could possibly already be levered 73 times even before it is tranched via a CDO.

Table 5.7: HG ABS CDO Asset Composition STL(X)

Security type	Rating	Percentage	STL(X)	Contribution
CDO	AAA	3.25%	48	0.72
	AA	2.00%	1000	7.40
	A	0.50%	2000	1.45
	BBB	0.50%	280	1.40
CLO	AAA	6.00%	7	0.42
	AA	5.00%	15	0.75
	A	5.25%	13	0.68
	BBB	4.50%	17	0.77
CMBS	AAA	16.00%	8	2.40
	AA	9.00%	50	13.50
	A	9.00%	30	9.00
	BBB	2.00%	65	6.00
CSO	AAA	2.00%	93	1.86
	AA	3.00%	93	2.79
	A	0.50%	93	0.47
Other CDO	AA	0.50%	1000	1.85
Prime RMBS	AA	2.00%	100	2.00
	A	3.00%	120	6.00
Subprime RMBS	AAA	9.00%	7	3.15
	AA	5.00%	40	10.00
	A	8.00%	76	31.20
	BBB	4.00%	85	16.00
Asset Composition STL(X)		100.00%		73.18

Next we see that while only 36% of the assets in the portfolio are rated AAA, we can convert them via correlation assumptions using securitisation models into a new vehicle where nearly 95% of the liabilities might be rated AAA (adding together the "width" percentages for tranches A, B and C in Table 5.8, which are all rated AAA, gives 94.47%). We have taken lower rated securities requiring higher capital and converted them into mainly very high rated securities requiring low capital.

Table 5.8: HG ABS CDO example

Tranche	Size (000s)	Subordination or attachment	Detachment	Width	Original rating	STL(0)	STL(X)
A	1,000,000	14.89%	100.00%	85.11%	AAA	1	73
B	75,000	8.51%	14.89%	6.38%	AAA	14.3	1046
C	35,000	5.53%	8.51%	2.98%	AAA	31.7	2315
D	30,000	2.98%	5.53%	2.55%	AA	38	2774
E	9000	2.21%	2.98%	0.77%	A	128	9320
F	3000	1.96%	2.21%	0.26%	A-	384	28032
G	15,000	0.68%	1.96%	1.28%	BBB	77.8	5679
SUB	8000	0.00%	0.68%	0.68%	NR	147	10722
Total	1,175,000						

This is really where we see the shadow banking system very clearly. We have turned mezzanine tranches of mostly consumer debt into mainly AAA-rated securities as though by alchemy. The reality is that there are assumptions on probabilities of default and correlations between those probabilities of default which are being highly levered. The issue is one of overconfidence in modelling, and overconfidence in maths and the ability to forecast defaults and correlations. The result is that we have a security levered over 2000 times rated AAA, and intended to be sold to the most conservative of investors. The top tranche is levered 73 times, but needs only 56bps in capital under Basel II rules.

The AAA rating alone is not sufficient to judge the riskiness of these securities. We should not assume that there may not theoretically be better measures than STL, but STL is an extremely simple, easily understood tool which explains the risk in these securities much better than the original ratings did.

Monoline insurer

As we saw in chapter three, monoline insurers issue financial guarantees to investors on securities assuring that their payments will be made in full and on time. Monoline insurers have typically been rated AAA as this then makes a conservative investor's investment decision easy. Monolines began in the 1970s primarily by writing financial guarantees on tax-exempt municipal debt.

There are literally tens of thousands of municipal bond issuers who issue tax-exempt debt. It would be difficult and inefficient for every issuer to directly address all possible investors for their debt as very often an issuer may have a very limited number of issues to issue. Likewise it is very inefficient for investors to get to know all of the tens of thousands of issuers, so investors need some way of quickly and easily deciding on whether to invest in an issue. Investors turned to rating agencies and monoline insurers to address this need. Rating agencies provide economies of scale by getting to know all the issuers, so investors do not have to do that cumbersome work.

> " A monoline insurance company exists to make investors' lives easier, especially those who want the very low risk historically associated with AAA ratings. "

Instead, investors can just refer to the issuer's rating from a rating agency and they can get a strong opinion on the likelihood an issuer will default. Likewise, if a rating is below AAA fewer investors will be interested in the paper and many will need to do more of their own due diligence for these riskier securities. The monoline insurers then do their due diligence (again providing a greater level of safety) and therefore provide the benefit of economies of scale to individual investors. An AAA rating has, in the past, always denoted a nearly riskless investment for any investor.

While the monoline insurers are licensed insurance companies and therefore are usually regulated by the state insurance commissioner within their own state, the rating agencies are in some sense their main regulator. In this context, a monoline insurance company exists to make investors' lives easier, especially conservative ones who want the very low risk historically associated with AAA ratings. These companies' franchises therefore are typically based on retaining AAA ratings so that they can easily stand between issuers wishing to sell paper and investors wanting safe investments.

However, in the 1990s monolines began guaranteeing structured credit products. These investments had high premiums and were not considered to be highly correlated with the creditworthiness of municipal issuers, providing diversification and growth in income. So a number of monoline insurers moved into the business of providing financial guarantees on highly-rated residential mortgage-backed paper and CDOs in order to broaden their business and increase their revenues.

As can be seen in Table 5.9, while the monoline insurers insured only highly-rated securities, they did so in a size much, much larger than their capital base and were extremely highly levered.

Table 5.9: leverage, or STL(X), of a stylised monoline insurance company

Monoline insurance company (US$m)

Insurance written	250,000		
		Avg STL(X)	Size times Avg STL(X)
Public finance	190,000	1	190,000
Subprime RMBS	10,000	12	120,000
ABS CDO	9000	73	657,000
Other	75,000	1	75,000
Total asset as per STL(X)			1,042,000
Statutory capital		2600	
Company STL(X)			401

What can be seen from this stylised example is that a monoline insurance company, even a leading one, might be able to lever itself massively using already levered securities and may still be able to retain its AAA rating, at least initially. We would argue that before having complete faith in a rating it could be helpful to ask:

What is the STL(X) of such a company?

Conclusions from the examples in this chapter

There are a number of conclusions we can draw from the examples in this chapter.

First, we saw how consumer debt and other lower-rated debt securities can be pooled into a portfolio which can be tranched into primarily AAA-rated securities via the mathematical assumption of less-than-perfect correlation. Essentially it is assumed that defaults will be less than perfectly correlated and therefore will be contained by the lower tranches in a structure.

Second, we saw how a large part of the process of securitisation and monoline insurance was about trying to get as much of the debt that needed to be funded for various assets to the AAA-rated level as possible, so that these investments are very desirable from a conservative investor's standpoint. The AAA rating is also a standard across many asset types, so that investors believe they are quickly and easily comparing relative safety between different asset classes.

It is also clear that ratings did not and do not measure the see-through leverage.

Ratings are not focused on the sensitivity to errors in underlying assumptions by rating agencies. Subprime borrowers with poor credit histories were issued mortgages, which were then securitised into home equity ABSs that were primarily rated AAA.

While AAA-rated auto loan, credit card and student loan backed securities may have STLs ranging from 1 to 3.5, the riskier or toxic AAA-rated securities typically have much higher leverage or STLs, some in the thousands.

AAA-rated subprime securities might have STLs of 20 to 30. AAA-rated corporate STCDOs might have STLs of 90 to 100. AAA-rated ABS CDO tranches might have STLs of 70 to over 2000 times.

That's right: 2000 times levered securities with the AAA rating.

The calculations of the stylised monoline company showed it to have an STL or leverage of over 400 times.

Rating agencies obviously believed the subordination of the securities held by monoline insurers was so high that extremely high leverage was acceptable. But if the AAA rating is all about safety, should securities with 70 to 2000 times leverage be rated AAA?

These findings make it clear: STL is orthogonal to ratings. Orthogonal factors are those which can be considered to be at 90 degree angles from one another on a Cartesian coordinate system. Imagine a plane with standard x and y axes.

If you know the x coordinate only, there is an infinite array of possibility for placing the object. Only when you know the y coordinate can you place the object exactly in its spot on the plane. Having a rating without the STL only gives you one of the coordinates you need to correctly place a security in the universe of risk. What we suggest is that in order to judge the risk of a security you must know its rating and its STL.

Another way to think of these measures is that STL is independent from ratings and vice versa; for any rating one can create a security with any STL and likewise for any STL one can create a security of any rating.

For example, take a BBB-rated portfolio of non-correlated assets and pool them into a portfolio without tranching. That portfolio would be rated BBB by definition. Also, assuming the underlying loans are not asset backed, the STL of that security would be 1. On the other hand, one could easily tranche that same portfolio, make the assumption that the assets are not highly correlated and find the level of subordination associated with an AAA security.

If one created a tranche for this same portfolio which attached at the lowest acceptable AAA attachment point and which detached at 100%, again one would have an STL 1 security. We have shown then how it would be possible to have a BBB-rated security with an STL 1 and an AAA-rated security with an STL 1.

Next we could also choose a tranche of an ABS CDO which attaches in the AAA-rated, no-loss, or low-expected-loss, zone. It might have an STL of 1000, as seen in the examples.

> **❝ Ratings and STLs are independent measures of risk: in order to judge the risk of a security you must know its rating *and* its STL. ❞**

This security may be safe if our predictions of losses and correlations are accurate and our calculations correct. However, as we have seen, a high level of precision is not generally possible, and the entire concept of correlation is not that robust. For these securities even a small error in our projections means they can become toxic and can quickly be completely wiped out.

Meanwhile, our examples of BBB-rated ABS CDO tranches are also shown to have very high STLs. We have seen then how we can have AAA assets with low or high STLs and we can have BBB-rated assets with low or high STLs, proof that ratings and STLs are independent measures of risk.

ABS tranches can be seen as out-of-the-money options

Another way of looking at these AAA-rated tranches of ABS securities is in terms of option calculations as far *out-of-the-money options*.

An *at-the-money option* is one whose strike price is equal to the current market price for the underlying. It has an implied **delta** (measurement of risk) of 50%, or may be thought of as having a similar riskiness to an investment in the underlying which is referenced by the option of 50%.

This is a reasonable assumption for small market movements. A far-out-of-the-money option may only have a delta of 1% of the underlying reference amount using a predetermined Gaussian structure of market price movements. An ABS security rated AAA then might be similar to a far-out-of-the-money option, having a very small delta for small market movements.

One of the main problems (others include continuous trading, normal markets, etc) for a VaR model is that it uses a Gaussian distribution, while market movements are known to be much fatter tailed or riskier than this. This presents difficulties when selling out-of-the-money options because the Gaussian distribution does not capture the fact that markets tend to trend.

This means that as long as the option remains out of the money, the delta is small and the reported VaR is small. The VaR hides the fact that if the expected distribution is wrong (as it generally is) the sold option may become at the money far sooner and more easily than imagined, and suddenly what appeared to be a very benign risk position grows 50-fold in delta risk terms.

Similarly, AAA-rated ABS tranches with high STLs change from being very low volatility securities to extremely high volatility securities as losses mount on the underlying loans. This phenomenon is typically referred to as being a very short gamma. High STL AAA-rated tranches of ABS securities are essentially far out of the money options and are extremely short gamma. This is why so many dealers who tried to use tools like ABX for hedging their positions were unable to manage their risk.

Assume for example that a CDO is made up of securities from the BBB-rated ABX index.[50]

If you own a super senior AAA-rated tranche of that CDO your delta would be very small as long as the implied losses on ABX were very low, or conversely

---

[50] The Markit ABX.HE index is a synthetic tradeable index referencing a basket of 20 subprime mortgage-backed securities.

as long as the prices of ABX were very high. If the implied losses in ABX began to rise, or in other words the price of ABX began to fall (as it did), the probability of default of your tranche would rise and you would have to sell more ABX as a hedge.

This massive negative gamma position is very difficult to manage and can create a self-feeding downward spiral of prices if many are using the same strategy. This is much like the portfolio insurance algorithms which caused the 1987 stock market crash. It was, of course, precisely this vicious cycle that took place during the credit crisis of 2007-2009. In essence, VaR type models are not appropriate for calculating risk of out-of-the-money options, especially for less liquid instruments, as they do not capture their negative gamma. This is the market-based measure equivalent to not capturing their STL.

In order to better understand the riskiness of an ABS, one must know not just its rating or the predicted loss distribution for a pool, but one must also know a tranche's sensitivity to errors in the loss distribution. One measure which captures this is STL.

6

Towards A Basel III

Chapter summary

Credit comes from the Latin root *credo*; to trust or to believe in.

In this chapter we will run through the accumulation of all of the flaws of the current risk measurement regimes which we have seen in earlier chapters and persuasively demonstrate that something must really change if we are to restore trust in the credit markets.

- Regulatory capital requirements are currently based on predictions of future price and loss distributions, which promotes cyclicality and optimisation based on those predictions.

- Optimisation of return on capital under this regime naturally increases leverage.

- This increase in leverage supports the creation of *Minsky moments* and Frederic Mishkin's *credit boom bubbles*, and worsens the impact of George Soros's *boom, bust processes*.

- Credit rating and VaR-based capital requirements, which are inherently based on predicted distributions, are therefore flawed.

- Using the STL family of risk indices in conjunction with predicted loss and price distributions to determine required capital will reduce the chance of bubbles and busts.

- Using STL will reduce the pro-cyclical nature of current capital regulations.

- Using STL in conjunction with ratings will help to indicate a rating's sensitivity to underlying model assumptions, massively improving any rating's usefulness.

Restoring confidence

We must restore confidence in our risk ratings of securities and our regulations, and belief in the safety of our banking system. Once we have done that we will have restored confidence and the flow of credit. The key to this, in our view, is to ensure that banks are never again so overly confident that they lever themselves excessively and that the leverage inherent in any investment becomes a standard risk parameter. We must use the family of STL risk indices to measure this risk and limit it in a way which helps to "stabilise the instability".[51]

This will mean a paradigm shift in the way risk is viewed, a paradigm shift in the way ratings agency ratings are viewed by investors and a paradigm shift in the way banks, investment banks and funds – in particular, money market funds – are regulated. Only when that has been achieved will we enjoy, without excessive worry, the return of an efficient global financial system even more reliable than that which fostered an unprecedented increase in productivity and prosperity, but ultimately broke down.

To recap a little: *what do the rating agencies do?*

The rating agencies are paid (and have been for decades) for playing the invaluable role of providing guidance on what is safe to invest in. As we showed earlier, this role is of major economic value in terms of economies of scale.

Though many may dispute this, we believe the global financial markets today are generally efficient and rating agencies are an important part of this efficiency. Modern portfolio theory has it that diversification is the only safe strategy for investors (assuming the risks are fairly priced and measured, and the concept not overly relied upon). Today, an individual investor has access to every type of fixed-income instrument available, allowing great diversification as long as the safety and price are fair. Rating agencies play the crucial role of determining that safety across the entire spectrum of available credit products.

The wise use of rating agencies then, if their ratings are accurate, should help investors achieve the maximum level of return for a given level of risk. Of course, for issuers and consumers this means a wise allocation of savings for the purpose of investment. When the ratings system works, it acts to optimise the economic system.

But as we all know, something went horribly wrong.

For asset-backed securities, again the rating agencies focused on using predicted loss distributions in order to rate the securities. Predictions of loss distributions were also used by regulators to measure unexpected losses and required capital for banks.

---

[51] Hyman P. Minsky, *Stabilizing an Unstable Economy* (McGraw Hill, 2008), p. 11.

But as it is difficult to predict loss distributions, you must know a security's or a bank's sensitivity to errors in a predicted loss distribution. By limiting sensitivity to errors in loss distributions we can create stronger, more robust and less optimised investment portfolios.

Let's take our ability to predict loss distributions to the extreme. Let's assume that we know a security's future loss distribution exactly and follow this approach to its logical conclusion.

Exploring extreme confidence and extreme leverage

Assume that a rating agency can determine ahead of time the exact loss distribution for a given class of securities with complete confidence.

This does not mean they would be able to determine exactly what loss might occur for those securities in the next year. Instead it would mean they could tell over a period of, for example, 52 years, exactly what set of losses would occur over that period. They might know, for example, that for 20 of the 52 years there would be no loss, for four years a 20bps loss, for four years a 30bps loss, for four years a 40bps loss, etc. It would be just like picking cards from a poker deck.

In this world where rating agencies have perfect pre-knowledge of the exact loss distribution – in the language of Robert Rubin, Alan Greenspan or Donald Rumsfeld – the agencies would have a complete knowledge of the known unknowns, there would be no unknown unknowns and they would know ahead of time that there will not be any black swans.

In this case, it is known exactly what the worst case will be and the amount of capital needed is very easy to determine. If a 1% spread can be earned on the entire pool of assets every year and the worst ever annual loss is 90bps, money would always be made on this investment. From the viewpoint of a bank's depositors the bank would always be safe. There would never be any need for any government bailouts.

Now imagine the point of view of bank shareholders. What should the bank's strategy be? What about regulators – how much capital should be required?

Bank shareholders are always looking to maximise their return on capital. Bank regulators want banks to be able to survive a 1000-year storm. Well, if a 1% spread can be earned per annum every year on this investment, the return will never be less than 10bps in any given year. So, why not lever 10 times? In that case the worst ever year will make ten times 10bps, or a 1% return on capital. In the best year there will be no losses so that ten times 1%, or a 10% return on capital, will be made. That is quite an impressive return.

But wait, perhaps more can be achieved. By levering 100 times, a minimum return on capital of 10% and a maximum return of 100% can be earned per annum. The logical conclusion from this is that the shareholder in the fund or bank taking this strategy should seek infinite leverage and they will get an infinite return on capital.

In a short period of time, the owners of that bank will be extraordinarily wealthy. What about the bank regulator? If there is never any risk to the depositors in the bank, if the loss distribution is known with certainty, and especially if their regulations are based on the predicted loss distribution, the bank will be allowed infinite leverage. This is where our global banking system was headed.

The flaw of course is that the loss distributions are not known and the sensitivity to errors in loss distribution predictions was not measured. As such, depositors were put at risk.

Let's next imagine a world where unlimited funds could be lent for a given area of investment based on this model, say the residential housing market. Imagine unlimited cheap financing for houses just for the application of a mortgage.

What might happen?

Simple microeconomics tells us the answer. The increase in financing available relative to unchanged demand for it might cause a drop in the cost of that financing. Even more important, an increase in demand for financial assets might reduce loan underwriting standards, allowing far more leverage by borrowers.

Taking our simple model another step then, once all the demand is met at a 1% spread by the banks, it might be necessary to reduce the spread to 90bps. After all, the bank will still make money every year (the loss distribution is known) and if the bank levers itself, it will do well. In addition, the bank might decide that it can still lend safely with an even smaller down payment than normal, say 10% rather than 20%.

From the point of view of the bank regulator, as the loss distribution is known, the bank will never go bust. The bank will make money every year. In fact, one can know exactly how much they will make over every 52-year period.

When the price of mortgages is decreased more people can afford homes, which means demand for homes will increase relative to supply and home prices increase. As the lending spread is lowered, and as more buyers become eligible to buy homes, due to reduced underwriting standards, house prices rise.

Then what happens?

Everyone will realise what is going on – investing in houses is a totally safe proposition because prices always rise. There may be evidence of a historical precedent in this area, suggesting that this had been tried before and it resulted in the whole financial system being damaged, but this would be ignored as confidence in the predicted loss distribution is unyielding.

Investing in houses might be seen as more stable than in the past, and investors might then become confident that the loss distribution has changed and that actually, the losses will be even less than previously thought. Investors might even come to believe that investing in housing is risk-free. If so, then maximising leverage is the only rational thing to do.

If investors take this next step, of course, what they might discover is that there are a lot of empty homes as they were purchased purely as financial speculation, and never were to be used for living in. It might then be discovered that the loss distribution in which so much faith had been placed was actually wrong and the housing market implodes.

In a *Financial Times* article of November 2009, Frederic Mishkin, a former Federal Reserve Board Governor, examined this type of phenomena.[52] He described two different types of bubbles. One is a "pure irrational exuberance bubble" in which prices rise beyond their economic value, but without an excessive increase in leverage. He gives the example of the prices of tech stocks in the late 1990s, from which, in retrospect, the economy rebounded surprisingly easily.

He also describes the most dangerous type of bubble; what he calls "a credit boom bubble". This is a "situation in which exuberant expectations about economic prospects or structural changes in financial markets lead to a credit boom. The resulting increased demand for some assets, raises their price and in turn encourages further lending against these assets, increasing demand, and hence their prices, even more, creating a positive feedback loop. This feedback loop involves increasing leverage, further easing of credit standards, then even higher leverage, and the cycle continues."

---

[52] Frederic Mishkin, *Financial Times*, 10/11/2009.

One could stop this cycle by measuring and limiting leverage, by measuring and limiting STL.

Returning to the existing problem

The rating agencies did not account for the possibility of a break in this cycle when we look at the housing market. They did not account for the possibility of generally falling house prices because it had not happened since the Great Depression. House prices began to fall and the losses on mortgage securities were beyond anything the rating agencies expected. People sent their house keys to the bank, the banks tried to sell. Excess supplies of homes for sale meant prices dropped, which hurt home owners. This caused more defaults. Selling begat lower prices, which begat further selling, and the banks and funds who lent the money for the mortgages went bust, leaving regulators wanting to know who was to blame.

Depositors at the affected banks and money market fund investors became scared and there was a run.

The basic flaw in the whole system was the assumption that the loss distribution of a set of credit assets can be known ahead of time with a high degree of confidence. In reality there is massive uncertainty around the predicted loss distributions. Even if a loss distribution has been very stable for a long period, using that knowledge itself may change the dynamics of the system and the future loss distributions. Therefore, the exact shape and nature of the loss distribution cannot be known ahead of time and this means leverage needs to be limited.

We think this phenomenon is exactly what Hyman Minsky was referring to in some of his writings. In his words:

> Any transitory tranquillity is transformed into an expansion in which the speculative financing of positions and the external financing of investment increase. An investment boom that strips the liquidity and increases the debt-equity ratios for financial institutions follows.

> Whether the break in the boom leads to a financial crisis, debt deflation and depression, or to a non-traumatic recession, depends on the overall liquidity in the economy.[53]

---

[53] Minsky, *Unstable Economy*, p. 244.

A transitory period of stability may make investors overly confident in their ability to predict loss distributions, which leads to a levering of investment positions, and to an investment boom. That boom will then naturally lead to a bust.

This, it seems to us, is also very closely related to the wisdom of George Soros and his theory of reflexivity. He believes that our perceptions themselves can alter the future outcomes of the system, creating fat-tailed economic events. He wrote:

> There is a two-way reflexive connexion between perception and reality which can give rise to initially self-reinforcing but eventually self-defeating boom-bust processes, or bubbles.[54]

Our belief in a reality of continuously rising prices leads to increased investment and increased leverage, which is finally seen to have been flawed, then leading to a bust, and a new belief in continuously falling prices.

High confidence in a future price or loss distribution leads to high leverage, in a self-feeding reflexive manner, until overbuilding is extreme, and the unexpected black swan appears.

In the language of Greenspan, Rubin and Rumsfeld, then, there are and must be unknown unknowns in our loss distribution. The future will not simply be a repeat of the past – like drawing cards by chance out of a deck – but instead there will be cards in the deck that are different from any of those ever drawn. The loss distribution cannot be known a priori with certainty. Therefore, banks must ensure that they are prepared for the unknown unknowns.

It is necessary to create firewalls between the financial system and the crises which can and will occur when market events take place that are unlike any of those which have been predicted. It is a matter of ensuring one financial institution cannot infect other institutions and bring them down. It is a matter of ensuring banks and borrowers are not

> **If the STL throughout the financial system is limited, financial risk associated with unexpected busts is reduced.**

excessively levered. It is about measuring and limiting the leverage – the fuel of any financial crisis – throughout the financial system.

---

[54] George Soros, *The New Paradigm For Financial Markets* (Public Affairs, 2008), p. x.

It must be ensured that the system is not overconfident or overly sensitive to its expectations of future loss distributions, and can survive unexpected events. It must be ensured that the sensitivity to errors in expectations is acceptable. The see-through leverage in banks, funds, money market funds, and throughout the financial system must be limited. If the amount of leverage is limited, the amount of funding available to fuel asset bubbles is also limited, and the financial risk associated with unexpected busts is reduced.

The flaws of Basel II

As we discussed earlier, Basel II capital requirements for ABS are based upon the rating of those securities which are in turn based upon predicting a loss distribution for the underlying assets within the ABS pool.

As all investment-grade securities are expected to have very small losses their ratings are based on estimating correctly the likelihood of highly unlikely events. The credit crisis has taught us that for certain structures, this approach does not work.

One of the reasons for the speed in the deterioration in the financial system was that very highly ratings-optimised slices of ABS were very sensitive to errors in the predictions of the pool loss distribution. So we have a two-fold problem:

1.   It is very difficult to predict the probability of highly unlikely events, especially when they are based on social phenomenon such as house prices.

2.   We have a situation where, due to very high STLs, certain securities have extreme risk.

If the subordination below these securities for some reason gets wiped out, they themselves are quickly wiped out. Instead of being robust, even in the case of protection being removed, they collapse. These optimised securities can move from AAA-rated to zero value very quickly. STL gives you a hint as to a security's level of optimisation. If it is highly optimised, then small errors can cause a dramatic fall in its rating, a dramatic rise in its capital requirement and a dramatic fall in its value.

If a bank has a very high confidence in the future loss distribution, and if that distribution is pretty stable and predictable, the bank is best served by leveraging infinitely in order to achieve the highest possible return on capital. As ratings-based capital rules under Basel II allow extremely high leverage they are flawed.

Next we will examine why, for the same reasons, VaR-based capital rules are also flawed.

The flaw in VaR-based capital rules

Assume a tranche of an asset-backed security attaches at 6% and detaches at 9%. This means that any losses in the asset pool up to 6% will be fully absorbed by the investors who own the 0% to 6% tranches. Losses in the assets of less than 6% will have zero impact on your investment, so your investment is said to have a zero change or delta with respect to losses at that level. But what happens if losses reach a bit higher, say from 6% to 7%?

As explained earlier, at this point the change in value effect or delta rises dramatically and your risk essentially explodes. You go from a one percentage point change in loss from 5% to 6% having zero impact on the value of your investment to a one percentage point loss from 6% to 7% wiping out 33% of your investment. This change in impact or change in delta is known in markets as being very *short gamma*.

Being very short gamma means that the calculated VaR for a position will be highly sensitive to the chosen market-based price or loss distribution. If the VaR price distribution never includes a scenario which touches the risk cliff, the security will show very little risk. On the other hand, once the VaR distribution begins to account for the possibility of prices exceeding the risk cliff, the VaR has the potential to explode, massively increasing required capital.

The financial system should be very robust, not just for events that have occurred in the past but also for events that have not yet been experienced. It is like preparing for a once-in-a-1000-year earthquake. Maybe it should first be assumed that stress events are so bad that at a minimum, some losses to each security will occur. Maybe it needs to be known that the system will at least survive if a loss threshold is touched, that the system will survive the shock of this 'earthquake'.

> **" The STL family of risk indices measures the sensitivity of an institution to losses in the case of a catastrophic event. "**

Similarly, maybe capital rules should not be based just on a confidence level around a set of unlikely scenarios, but should also be based on the sensitivity of an institution to losses in the case of a catastrophic event. The STL family of risk indices is a set of measures of this risk.

The flaws of money market regulations

Money market funds are of huge importance in the United States. According to SIFMA, at the end of 2008 there was more than $3.8 trillion held in money market mutual funds. Individuals typically use their money market accounts as their source of liquidity for everyday needs. Individuals can write cheques, pay bills electronically and go up to any ATM machine globally which accepts their bank's card and withdraw funds. People need this money to be in riskless investments. Safety and high liquidity is the key mantra for any money market fund manager.

Likewise, money market funds are used by small businesses as their current accounts. From their money market accounts small businesses meet their day-to-day cash needs, depositing funds received and making necessary payments. These are the same current or working capital accounts from which virtually all small businesses make their payroll payments to their employees.

> " Safety and high liquidity is the key mantra for any money market fund manager. "

While everyone likes to see their money working for them by getting a reasonable return or interest, including their money market funds, the reason for using money market funds is not to maximise return. People want to be able to withdraw funds as needed, especially in unexpected circumstances. Money market funds are all about safety and convenience.

Money market mutual funds in the United States are regulated by the Securities and Exchange Commission under the Investment Company Act of 1940. According to the SEC website:

> A money market fund is a type of mutual fund that is required by law to invest in low-risk securities. These funds have relatively low risks compared to other mutual funds and pay dividends that generally reflect short-term interest rates.[55]

---

[55] www.sec.gov/answers/mfmmkt.htm

Money market mutual funds invest in short-dated securities typically maturing in 90 days or less in order to ensure low risk and high liquidity. They are specifically regulated under rule 2A-7, which stipulates that all securities investments must have a maturity of less than 397 days and must achieve one of the top two ratings from a Nationally Recognised Statistical Rating Organisation (NRSRO), or must be of equivalent quality.

Moody's and Standard & Poor's both have a special ratings scale specifically for money market instruments. Standard & Poor's uses the scale of A-1+ for the safest short-term rating, and then A-1, A-2, A-3 and so on. Similarly, Moody's uses P-1 for the safest paper, then P-2, P-3 and so on.

Money market mutual funds do their best to maintain an exact US$1.00 share price, but pay regular dividends. As the main interest of money market investors is safety and convenience, these funds typically do not reach for yield by increasing risks. For borrowers, as there is a deep pool of such funds, if you meet their strict criteria you can achieve the cheapest possible funding levels.

For financial engineers making paper 2A-7 eligible means cheap funding. In order to take advantage of this, financial engineers built much of the shadow banking system around asset-backed commercial paper (ABCP) that was 2A-7 eligible.

CDOs issued highly-rated ABCP to fund the super senior tranches. Structured investment vehicles issued ABCP. In some countries corporate synthetic obligations (CSOs) or corporate single tranche CDOs issued short-term commercial paper for money market funds. All of these issues would achieve the highest ratings from the rating agencies as their expected losses based upon the historical stress tests would imply no or nearly no losses.

What is wrong with this?

As we know, expected losses are based on history and large numbers of assumptions embedded in ratings models such as correlation of time to default. The complexity and sensitivity of these ratings to the underlying assumptions is an important measure which is not directly captured in the ratings or in 2A-7 rules.

This sensitivity or risk can be captured, of course, through STL. The importance of cheap funding and the ability of 2A-7 funds to provide cheap funding meant it was natural that financial engineers would design paper specifically to meet the needs of 2A-7 funds.

Now that we have STL and we have calculated it for a number of shadow banking securities types, we see that the ABCP of CDO tranches rated AAA, or A-1 or A-1+ short term may have had STLs of 120 to 3000. Paper levered 3000 times does not meet the needs of investors for a safe place to store their everyday money.

> " ABCP of CDO tranches rated AAA, A-1 or A-1+ may have had STLs of 120 to 3000. This does not meet the need of investors for a safe place to store their money. "

For SIVs, as we have seen, the ABCP might have an STL of 40 or more. STLs for CSOs with the highest possible ratings might be 90 or more.

It is not surprising then that in 2008, when underlying historical loss distributions proved completely unreliable, the shadow banking system – which relied so heavily on these historical distributions and levered investments tens, hundreds and thousands of times in AAA, and A-1+ rated securities – was struck by panic. Funds to be taken out of the ATM machine to buy groceries, and funds used by small businesses to meet payroll, were now at risk. There was a run on money market funds.

On 16 September 2008 the oldest money market mutual fund 'broke the buck' – meaning its NAV fell below $1 per share – as it dropped to 97 cents. Within days, a number of funds were breaking the buck and, as panic ensued, investors withdrew funds en masse.

On 17 September institutional investors withdrew a net $179 billion from money market mutual funds and piled into US treasury bills. The collapse in deposits and panic from investors meant that funds would need to sell assets at firesale prices, which would cause more losses, more panic and then more selling. This would represent a vicious collapse of a fund's product built for safety and liquidity, and regulated by the SEC.

Wanting to avoid a collapse of the US financial system and wanting to avoid a world panic similar to that of the 1930s, the US government stepped in to support money market mutual funds. On 19 September 2008 the US Treasury department announced a voluntary guarantee programme for money market mutual funds similar to that of the FDIC insurance for bank deposits. It was intended to stop the vicious cycle in its tracks and restore confidence to those investing in these vehicles.

What Basel III might look like

The **Bank for International Settlements** (BIS) is sometimes known as the central bankers' bank. Under the guise of the BIS, central bankers meet to discuss current events and practices that will best support the global financial system. As all central banks are trying to achieve the same goals, an atmosphere of cooperation dominates. In that vein the BIS formed what is known as the Committee on the Global Financial System (CGFS). The CGFS was established by the governors of the G10 central banks on 8 February 1999.

According to the BIS website the committee's primary objectives are the following:

- To seek *to identify and assess potential sources of stress* in the global financial environment through a regular and systematic monitoring of developments in financial markets and systems, including through an evaluation of macroeconomic developments;

- To further the understanding of the functioning and underpinnings of financial markets and systems through a *close monitoring of their evolution and in-depth analyses*, with particular reference to the implications for central bank operations and broader *responsibilities for monetary and financial stability*;

- To promote the development of *well-functioning and stable financial markets* and systems through an examination of alternative policy responses and the elaboration of corresponding policy recommendations.

  In its analysis, the committee *should pay particular attention to the nexus between monetary and financial stability*, to the linkages between institutions, infrastructures and markets, to the actual and potential changes in financial intermediation and to the incentive structures built into markets and systems.

The committee should clearly be monitoring potential sources of stress, analysing the evolution of markets, and promoting financial stability. All of these roles can be enhanced by using the new language of risk we have introduced in this book, and in particular by using the STL family of risk indices.

The response of the CGFS to the crisis

In July 2008, in response to the financial crisis which began in the summer of 2007, the CGFS published a paper entitled 'Ratings in structured finance: what went wrong and what can be done to address shortcomings?'.

The paper is based on an extensive study of rating agencies, investors and regulators around the globe and it examines what went wrong in the financial system which caused the crisis. As the core of the shadow banking system was the cause of the collapse and as that system was and is for all practical purposes regulated by the rating agencies and their ratings, the paper focuses on what it calls the credit rating agencies (CRAs).

The paper focuses on how the CRAs underestimated the severity of the housing market downturn and how they were using limited historical data which added to rating model risk. CRAs overall had underestimated risks. The paper further describes, as we have in this book, the widespread use of ratings by issuers, investors and regulators in determining risk across different types of securities. Moreover, the paper looks at how house price estimates and refinancing assumptions were all overly optimistic. It looks at monoline insurance companies and their heavily ratings-dependent business models. It examines the ratings models for SIVs and what went wrong.

Most importantly, in its analysis it searches for how the global central banks might better measure and regulate risks in order to ensure that a financial crisis such as that we have experienced can be avoided in the future.

In particular, among its recommendations it suggests that:

> CRAs should document the sensitivity of SF (structured finance) tranche ratings to changes in their central assumptions regarding default rates, recovery rates and correlations. Where only limited historical data on underlying asset pools are available, this should be clearly disclosed as a source of model risk, as should any adjustments to mitigate the risk.

At the conclusion of its executive summary, it states:

> With respect to the question of how the rating risk of SF products can be better captured or differentiated from that of plain vanilla credit instruments, one view expressed by some institutional investors and CRAs was that alternative rating scales for SF products may be costly and could create confusion among users of ratings information.

At the same time, the provision of more information and of additional indicators that capture rating risk was supported by both investors and CRAs themselves.

We propose that one candidate for these additional indicators of rating risk is, of course, the STL family of risk indices.

The paper focuses on "improving information available on key risk factors that drive SF ratings, in particular on model risk and the sensitivity of ratings to assumptions about macroeconomic developments". This is simply and easily captured by the STL family of risk indices.

Tables 6.1 and 6.2 are adopted from the GCFS report and form a well thought-out framework for delineating the choices available for differentiating ratings on SF assets in order to better measure risk. For each class of possible additional indicators the framework examines how they might work, how difficult they may be to calculate and how they might be used. This gives us an opportunity to use their framework to evaluate how well or poorly STL might fit as an additional indicator to ratings.

Table 6.1: options for differentiating SF and single-name borrower ratings[56]

	Example	Concept	Analytical requirements
One-dimensional measures			
Notching	SF product is rated A instead of AAA.	Applying lower rating to capture greater tail risk or model risk.	High. Estimate of full loss distribution required.
Separate rating scale	1, 2, 3 instead of AAA, AA, A.	Information of unexpected losses of SF is embedded in new rating scales.*	High[57]. Estimate of full loss distribution required, subject to model risk, short data history etc.
Fixed asset class suffix	AAA.sf instead of AAA.	Suffix added to existing rating indicates different loss characteristics of asset class.	Relatively low. Need to identify SF asset class.
Two-dimensional measures			
Simple risk suffix	AAA.h, AAA.c, AAA.nr instead of AAA.	Suffix indicates whether risk of downgrade of SF instrument is higher (h) or comparable (c) to single-name products, or whether risk cannot be rated (nr), in the case of new instruments with high model uncertainty.	Medium. Requires understanding of broad risk categories.
Ordinal risk suffix	AAA.v1, AAA.v2, etc.	Information on unexpected loss (volatility) or measure of tail risk (eg. on multi-notch transitions).	High. Estimate of full loss distribution required. Subject to model risk, short data history, etc.
Rating confidence suffix (could be combined with risk suffix or shown separately)	AAA.c1, AAA.c2, etc.	Information on uncertainly resulting from model risk (including parameter uncertainty, confidence about quality of input information, etc).	Medium to high, depending on granularity of confidence suffix.
Multidimensional measures	AAA.v1.q1, AAA.v2.c3.q1, etc.	Information on a number of risk measures, such as volatility, rating confidence, and quality of input parameters in the model.	High. Estimate of full loss distribution required.

---

[56] Simplified exposition.

[57] Assumes that the separate rating scale would incorporate information on the credit loss distribution of SF instruments – say, unexpected loss – in addition to the information contained in the existing rating when calibrating the SF rating scale. Otherwise, the separate rating scale would just be a change in the nomenclature, and essentially no different from an asset class suffix.

Table 6.2: effectiveness of SF rating risk indicators in meeting different objectives[58]

	Would indicator trigger a review of investment mandates?	Would indicator clearly convey information on rating risk?	Would indicators reduce risk-taking by uninformed investors?	Would indicators allow comparison of rating risk across SF instruments?
One dimensional measures				
Notching	Unlikely.	No.	Investors should be discouraged by lower spreads for stated rating.	Not explicitly.
Separate rating scale	Yes. Investors would be forced to rewrite mandates.	No. No distinction between rating and risk.	Yes, at least implicitly.	Yes, at least implicitly.[59]
Fixed asset class suffix	Perhaps investors might ignore suffix.	No. Only general indication that asset class is different.	Perhaps.	No. Risk difference across SF assets would not be captured.
Two-dimensional measures				
Simple risk suffix	More likely than for asset class suffix as investors will be alerted to risk levels.	Yes, in broad relative terms.	More likely, depending on adjustments made to investment guidelines.	Only in a relatively simplistic way.
Ordinal risk suffix	More likely than for asset class suffix as investors will be alerted to risk levels.	Yes.	More likely, depending on adjustments made to investment guidelines.	Yes.
Rating confidence suffix (could be combined with risk suffix or shown separately)	More likely than for asset class suffix as investors will be alerted to risk levels.	Yes, depending on the granularity of confidence scale.	More likely, depending on adjustments made to investment guidelines.	Yes, depending on the granularity of confidence scale.
Multidimensional measures	Likely.	Yes, but clarity might suffer with additional dimensions.	Likely, depending on adjustments made to investment guidelines.	Yes.

---

[58] Simplified exposition. Assumes that ratings depend on the methodology used to calculate risk indicators. For instance, volatility measures can be based on models or historical data.

[59] Assumes that the separate rating scale will incorporate information on dispersion of the credit loss distribution of SF instruments (see * in Table 6.1).

How STL can be used

STL could be deployed as a single dimensional rating which is used as part of the current rating scale. This could be, for instance, to redefine the ratings concept for asset-backed securities to include not just expected losses or probabilities of the first dollar of loss but also a maximum for STL for each rating class.

This would mean that there would also be a maximum sensitivity to changes in the expected loss at the point subordination is eliminated. Alternatively, STL can be used as a measure of sensitivity to errors in model or underlying loss distributions.

As we have seen, STL did a much better job all alone of estimating the future ratings of asset-backed securities than did the original ratings themselves. If the CRAs wish to include this in the current rating scale, it would meet a number of the criteria set out as important by the CGFS.

> **If the CRAs wish to include STL in the current rating scale, it would meet a number of the criteria the CGFS set out as important.**

Another possible use for STL could be as a second indicator to be used in conjunction with the current expected loss-based framework. This, we think, would be a superior approach; STL and expected loss are really two separate dimensions.

As explained earlier, STL can be considered to be orthogonal to the current rating method or expected loss approach. That being the case, there is true value added by using both indicators separately. STL again is sensitivity to an error in the underlying loss distribution, whereas ratings are based upon expected loss given an assumed or predicted future loss distribution. In that way, to the extent that the predictions of future loss distributions are accurate, ratings tell you all about the expected losses. STL tells you about how sensitive you are to errors in those predictions.

A third possibility could be to add further dimensions to these first two. One potential additional measure which may be useful is one telling you about the volatility of historical loss distributions for a particular class, or how limited the historical information available for an asset class is.

Table 6.3 provides an evaluation of how STL might apply to the CGFS framework.

Table 6.3: an evaluation of the effectiveness of STL as a risk rating indicator in meeting the CGFS objectives[60]

	Would indicator trigger a review of investment mandates?	Would indicator clearly convey information on rating risk?	Would indicator reduce risk-taking by uninformed investors?	Would indicator allow compliance of rating risk across SF instruments?
One-dimensional measures				
STL as second factor in current rating scale	Yes	Yes	Yes	Yes
STL as a separate rating scale	Yes	Yes	Yes	Yes
Two-dimensional measures				
STL as an additional dimensional measure of risk	Yes	Yes	Yes	Yes
Multidimensional measures				
STL included with ratings and other orthogonal risk measures	Yes	Yes	Yes	Yes

Table 6.3 was created by taking Table 6.2, which contains the desirable objectives of SF risk indicators as suggested by the CFGS, and inputting our own judgement as to the validity of using STL as a risk indicator. As can be seen, STL could be very useful as an indicator for the investing and financial regulating communities, especially since it is incredibly simple to calculate.

---

[60] This is a very subjective use of the CGFS' table.

Conclusion: Towards Basel III

To sum up how far we have come in these pages we should go over once more what happened and how we might avoid it taking place again.

A summary of what this book has covered

Capital requirements for banks are all about having enough capital to survive unexpected losses. Banks are, in general, required under banking regulations to have enough capital in order to withstand extreme cyclical and idiosyncratic loss scenarios. It would be typical for banks to be required to be able to withstand 99.9% of all imaginable scenarios for any one-year period. But clearly all of those rules broke down as financial institution after financial institution failed, or required additional capital, across the globe.

The FDIC reported at the beginning of 2006 that it had only minimal risk in the system of banks it covered with only $4 billion of assets at banks considered troubled, the lowest it had been in many years. Then in the third quarter of 2008 the amount of assets at institutions considered troubled jumped to $117 billion.

In the fourth quarter of 2008 things were so bad for banks that the FDIC offered to provide guarantees for bank bonds in order to ensure they had sufficient access to liquidity, as the banking system appeared to be on the verge of collapse. In the first quarter of 2009 it had the greatest number of failures of banks covered by its insurance scheme since 1992.

Bank failures were rife in 2008. Actual or near failures of financial institutions included Washington Mutual, IndyMac, Northern Rock, Sachsen LB, IKB, HRE, Countrywide Financial, Lehman Brothers, Bear Stearns, Fannie Mae and Freddie Mac. Governments from around the world quickly went from strong confidence in their well-capitalised and highly-regulated banking systems to complete panic.

Regulators, using their best analytical resources and measures, had still made errors. The global system was impacted, we would argue, in part because of a conceptual error made not only by regulators, but also investors, bankers and rating agencies.

Basel II in particular required minimum capital requirements for asset-backed securities based upon ratings for ABSs held in banking books and value at risk (VaR) for trading books.

The problem for both of these concepts with regard to ABS is the same. For AAA-rated ABS, as long as the predicted future loss distribution for the underlying assets remains unchanged or nearly unchanged, the volatility of the prices for those securities will likely remain very low. But untested mortgage types and a bull market in house prices that lasted decades meant that the historical data was useless for predicting what would happen.

Low historical price volatility meant very little capital would be required to keep these assets on trading books under Basel II capital rules. Buying protection from AAA-rated insurance companies or AAA-rated monoline insurers on these AAA-rated ABSs meant that traditionally measured risk would be extremely negligible.

Likewise, for banking-book risk Basel II introduced capital requirements which were based on ratings or the expectation of loss given a certain confidence interval using a predicted loss distribution. As shown earlier, AAA-rated senior tranche securities of ABS required only 7% of 8%, or 56 basis points, of capital. The problem here is that if an investment is highly sensitive to errors in the predicted loss distribution, and those predictions are unreliable, the capital requirement will be far too low.

> **STL measures the sensitivity of an asset to changes in the underlying loss distribution at the point where the subordination is exhausted; it is a measure of sensitivity to catastrophe.**

Minimum capital requirements should be in part based on the potential volatility of predicted loss distributions and their impact on expected losses. Therefore a measure of sensitivity to changes in predicted loss distributions is needed. The family of STL risk indices offers such a measure.

STL measures the sensitivity of an asset to changes in the underlying loss distribution at the point where the subordination is exhausted. In essence it is a measure of sensitivity to catastrophe. This is in a sense a simple extension of the old capital rules used for banks before Basel I and before the use of securitisation as a financing tool. Under the old method, 8% capital or a maximum of 12 times leverage was allowed. More simply, maybe banks should be limited by a maximum STL, as opposed to a maximum nominal leverage.

Under Basel II banks filled their coffers with 50 to 3000 times levered securities with AAA ratings which required 56 to 96bps in capital. While the expected losses were small, a catastrophic error in the predictions of losses meant that banks would quickly be wiped out. And that is exactly what happened. When house prices stopped rising and assets began to experience unexpected declines the entire banking system became immediately at risk.

Basel III ought to include a measure of sensitivity to errors in predicted loss distributions such as STL in order to ensure sufficient capital is applied to highly-levered securities.

The two most prominent criticisms of current bank capital rules

Finally, the most popular criticisms around the current bank capital rules appear to be that, firstly, the required regulatory capital stipulated by the rules was simply too low and, secondly, that they are too pro-cyclical. By adopting capital rules based on STL, both of these issues would be directly addressed.

On the first point, the required regulatory capital associated with high STL, AAA-rated securities was too low. We hope that it is clear from this exposition, and will become clearer still through further work others will perform in the future, that very high sensitivity to model risk and therefore high sensitivity to errors in predicted future loss distributions would mean higher capital requirements. One judge of this sensitivity is STL.

Under such a system ABS CDOs would have required the highest amount of capital of any asset class we have examined. AAA-rated super senior ABS CDO tranches might have STLs in the area of 75, or leverage of 75 times, and when we regress STL against current ratings we get an STL associated with CCC-rated assets. Given that, higher capital requirements seem only reasonable.

What are the practical implications of these views?

ABS CDOs would likely never have been invented. Buying protection from AAA-rated insurance and AAA-rated monoline insurance companies who wrote heavy amounts of ABS and ABS CDO protection would have had no impact on capital requirements. Equally, credit protection purchased from credit derivative product companies who wrote protection on AAA-rated ABS CDO tranches would have had no beneficial impact on capital requirements either.

If STL were to be adopted, AAA-rated ABS CDO and AAA-rated corporate CSO tranches would never be found in money market funds. SIV commercial paper would be thought about much longer and harder before ever being allowed into money market funds.

Overall, it can be seen that many of the problems which plagued bank capital since the beginning of this crisis could have been avoided.

The second area of contention with current bank capital rules is that they are very cyclical, as ratings have fallen in unison across credit assets as the global economy went into recession. But what we see with STL is an indicator which is not dependent on estimating the loss distribution and therefore is not subject to drift due to those specific circumstances over time.

The STLs we have presented are the STLs as they would have stood on the day the securities were issued, which is the same as the STLs as they stand today. Basing bank capital rules on stable STLs would mean far more stable capital requirements across the business cycle.

Restoring confidence with STL

One of the authors originally began thinking at the suggestion of a friend about how one might create a measure, using the experience we now have, which could differentiate between the toxic AAA-rated assets and safe AAA-rated assets; a measure that would address all the concerns of investors and regulators which have come about during this, the worst financial crisis in decades; a measure that would explain the housing bubble and the blow up of the financial system; a measure that could be implemented to ensure that such a crisis would never happen again; and above all a measure which would help to *restore confidence* in our financial system. Our answer to that call is STL.

Glossary

asset-backed commercial paper (ABCP) – Short-term debt, typically less than one year in maturity, issued by a special purpose corporation to fund other debt assets, such as mortgages, auto loans, equipment leases or credit cards. ABCP is issued by structured investment vehicles, commercial paper conduits and collateralised debt obligations. The primary source of repaying ABCP is typically the asset pool owned by the special purpose corporation issuing the commercial paper.

asset-backed security (ABS) – A debt security of any maturity issued by a special purpose corporation in order to fund pools of smaller, typically less liquid loans. The payments on an asset-backed security are typically fully dependent upon cash flows from the underlying assets. Examples of asset pools include mortgages, credit card receivables and auto loans. ABSs often have fairly homogeneous pools of assets.

Bank for International Settlements (BIS) – An international organisation which fosters international monetary and financial cooperation and serves as a bank for central banks (www.bis.org).

collateralised debt obligation (CDO) – A special purpose corporation which purchases securities and loans and issues tranched liabilities to fund those assets. The pool of assets is often non-homogeneous, and may contain ABS securities, or other CDO securities. They are called *collateralised* as the assets form the collateral which is used to pay off the liabilities.

collateralised loan obligation (CLO) – A CDO whose collateral pool is made up of primarily corporate loans, usually leveraged loans.

commercial paper (CP) – A short-term debt obligation typically of less than one year in maturity, used to fund short-term credit needs, such as inventories, or as in the case of ABCP, other debt obligations.

credit-linked note (CLN) – A note, typically issued by a bank, whose repayment is linked not just to the bank, but also to the creditworthiness of a reference entity, usually a corporation or government. If the reference entity experiences a default during the life of the CLN, the investor will typically incur the loss from the default event. If no default event occurs, the investor typically gets paid back in full.

credit rating agency (CRA) – A company that issues credit ratings for debt issued by corporations, governments and special purpose corporations. A CRA may issue a rating for an issuer and for different types of debt issued by an issuer.

enhanced see-through leverage ESTL(X) (patent pending) – A new risk index calculated by multiplying the leverage of a borrower by the see-through leverage (STL(X)) of the issuing lender.

delta – A mathematical term meaning change. Typically the first derivative, or the rate of change of one variable with respect to another variable, is referred to as the delta of one variable with respect to the other. For example, if we have the equation $y = 4x$, we know that y changes by four units (or has a delta of four) for every one unit that x changes by. STL(X) or see-through leverage is an estimate of the delta, or rate of change, of the value of a security with respect to the base underlying assets to which it refers, or supports with capital, at the point where a loss is initially incurred by the security itself.

Gaussian distribution – A theoretical frequency distribution representing the values a variable may take on. It is symmetrical and bell shaped, and also known as a normal distribution. Its creation is attributed to Carl Friedrich Gauss.

high grade – A debt security whose credit rating is at least investment grade, or greater than BBB-.

mezzanine – A debt security which falls in seniority between equity and the most senior debt within a corporate liability capital structure.

modern portfolio theory (MPT) – A theory generally attributed to Harry Markowitz which looks to maximise the return on a portfolio of assets for a given level of risk, assuming assets are less than perfectly correlated, and assuming asset returns are well described by Gaussian or normal distributions.

money market – The market for short-term debt obligations typically maturing in less than one year, including bank deposits, repurchase agreements and commercial paper.

non-accelerating inflation rate of unemployment (NAIRU) – The theoretical equilibrium unemployment rate for a given economy at which inflation neither rises nor falls.

over the counter (OTC) – The market for transactions which occur between counterparts that do not happen on an exchange nor through a clearing house.

return on assets (ROA) – The total return achieved on a set of assets, typically in annualised terms.

return on capital (ROC) – The total return achieved on a given capital base, typically in annualised terms.

residential mortgage-backed security (RMBS) – A debt security or asset-backed security (ABS) whose repayment is based upon the performance of a specified pool of residential mortgages.

risk-weighted asset (RWA) – The assets of a financial institution weighted by credit riskiness as per Basel regulations, used to determine the capital adequacy of an institution.

shadow banking system – The system of non-bank financing entities and tools which has grown dramatically since the late 1980s. The coining of the term is often attributed to Paul McMulley of PIMCO. The shadow banking system consists of SIVs, commercial paper conduits, CDOs, monoline insurers, credit derivative product companies and other vehicles.

special purpose entity (SPE) – Sometimes referred to as a special purpose vehicle (SPV), this is a corporation set up for a specific purpose, usually for the purchasing of certain assets and the issuing of certain liabilities.

special purpose vehicle (SPV) – See **special purpose entity (SPE)**.

simple tranche leverage STL(0) (patent pending) – A member of the family of STL risk measures for tranches of ABS securities. It is calculated as follows:

$$\text{Simple tranche leverage, or STL}(0) = \frac{(100\% - \text{tranche attachment }\%)}{(\text{tranche detachment} - \text{tranche attachment})}$$

see-through leverage STL(X) (patent pending) – A member of the family of STL risk measures, which approximates the sensitivity of a tranche investment to a one-basis-point change in the assumed losses in the underlying reference loan portfolios at the point where subordination is wiped out.

structured finance collateralised debt obligation (SFCDO) – A CDO whose underlying asset pool consists of ABSs and CDOs.

structured investment vehicle (SIV) – A SIV was a special purpose vehicle which purchased assets and funded those assets by issuing ABCP, medium-term notes and income notes. SIVs were different from ABCP conduits in that they typically had larger capital support from income notes, funding in the form of medium-term notes, and creditworthiness typically based upon the market value of the underlying assets.

tranche – A liability issued by an asset-backed security that represents a defined slice of the capital structure funding the asset-backed vehicle.

tranche attachment point – The amount of subordination below a given tranche of a capital structure, usually given in terms of percentage of total capital. The attachment point may also be thought of as the point at which a given tranche attaches to the losses of the underlying asset portfolio.

tranche detachment point – The amount of capital determined by the subordination below a tranche plus the capital represented by the tranche itself, usually described as a percentage of total capital. It can also be thought of as representing the amount of losses of the asset pool at which point the tranche detaches from losses or is wiped out.

tranche width – The percentage of capital determined by the size of a tranche. Tranche width can be thought of as the tranche detachment point minus the tranche attachment point.

tranching – The slicing of a capital structure of an asset-backed security into tranches.

value at risk (VaR) – A measure of financial risk based upon the potential change of the market value of a portfolio of assets, given a defined time period and a defined confidence level based upon historical price changes and assuming a Gaussian distribution.

Bibliography

Books

Bookstaber, Richard, *A Demon Of Our Own Design* (John Wiley and Sons, 2007)

Ebenstein, Alan, *Friedrich Hayek: A Biography* (University of Chicago Press, 2001)

Galbraith, John Kenneth, *The Great Crash 1929* (Houghton Mifflin Company, 1954)

Greenspan, Alan, *The Age Of Turbulence* (The Penguin Group, 2007)

Lowenstein, Roger, *When Genius Failed* (Random House, 2000)

Mandelbrot, Benoit and Hudson, Richard L., *The (Mis)behaviour of Markets* (Basic Books, 2004)

Minsky, Hyman P., *Stabilizing an Unstable Economy* (McGraw Hill, 2008)

Ranelagh, John, *Thatcher's People: An Insider's Account of the Politics, the Power, and the Personalities* (HarperCollins, 1991)

Rubin, Robert E. and Weisberg, Jacob, *In An Uncertain World* (Random House, 2003)

Soros, George, *The New Paradigm For Financial Markets* (Public Affairs, 2008)

Tett, Gillian, *Fools' Gold* (Little, Brown, 2009)

Taleb, Nassim, *The Black Swan* (Penguin Books, 2007)

Newspapers and journals

Financial Times

New York Times

Stigletz, Joseph, 'Capitalist Fools', *Vanity Fair*, January 2009

Websites

www.bankofengland.co.uk/publications/speeches/2009/speech374.pdf

www.bis.org/publ/bcbs04a.pdf

www.bis.org/publ/plcy07q.pdf

www.bis.org/publ/bcbs23.pdf

www.defenselink.mil/transcripts/transcript.aspx?transcriptid=3490

www.federalreserve.gov/BoardDocs/Speeches/2004/20040103

www.moodys.com

www.reagan.utexas.edu/archives/speeches/1987/061287d.htm

www.sec.gov/answers/mfmmkt.htm

www.standardandpoors.com

Index

Page numbers in bold denote a glossary entry.